Feels Better. Flows Better.

Feng Shui for Inspired Living

By Kerri Miller

Feels Better. Flows Better./Kerri Miller. -- 2nd ed.

ISBN 978-0-9907449-1-7

Library of Congress Number 2016952665

Published by Feng Shui Pathways

DEDICATION

I dedicate this book to my family:

In memory of my mom, who I'm certain divinely guided this opportunity and writing process for me. And to my dad, who always and still encourages me not to quit anything that I start.

To my sister, for always going first and carving an easier path for me.

To my husband, Steve, who is my dearest love, my rock, and my eternal furniture mover and picture hanger.

And to my daughters, Casey and Haley, who are my deepest inspiration in everything that I do.

Thank you all.

Acknowledgements

There are so many people to thank for helping this book come together! First, it never would have materialized at all without the invitation from Jenny Thayer McKinney and Cedar Loft Publishing. Jenny encouraged me from the start and she and her team guided me gently through the entire writing and publishing process. I truly never would have done it if Jenny hadn't laid it out right in front of me!

I've always liked to write but I never considered myself a writer. Pumping out a quick article seems fairly easy to me, but linking all my thoughts and ideas into one long, sensible and interesting BOOK is much different!! I'm so grateful for having friends to reach out to when I got lost in the thick of it: Adele Miller took time out of her abundant life to review my drafts/outline/scribble and helped me find my way back to the vision. And Susan Woodrow took my piles of words that resembled straw and nudged me to spin them into a more gold-like substance. I would have thrown in the towel without these two kind and generous souls!

Although writing a book was intimidating, making it pretty with useful illustrations and photos was downright scary to me! Huge thanks go out to the people that helped me on this end: The talented Marty McCagg created all the beautiful graphics and laying out the book. Sarah Commerford accompanied me to several homes to take many of the photos highlighted. More home and landscape photos were contributed by Laurie Mounce and Jill Boylen. Seeing these graphics and pictures pop from the pages of my words makes me truly proud of the work!

I shared many examples in the book gathered by working with so many people that invited me in to Feng Shui their homes. I'm truly grateful for each experience and connection I make along the way and for the opportunity to share Feng Shui with you all. I'd like to give special thanks to those that gave me permission to share their stories and/or pictures of their homes. I know it will inspire others on their journey of change.

After my ideas and visions were all down on paper I solicited a few brave beta readers to review and apply this Feng Shui stuff! Thank you to Inge Daniels, Suzanne Becker and Tamara Church for giving me great feedback from the reader's perspective. They challenged me to think through each thought and lesson so it was user friendly. I'm so grateful for the clarity they helped weave into each part of the book.

Most especially, I appreciate all of the wonderful friends and family members that cheered and coaxed me on as I got to each of the "what on earth was I thinking" stages of writing and editing! There are too many of you too count but please know I'm grateful for each one of you.

Table of Contents

Introduction

When I was younger I loved to rearrange my bedroom – often! Like most youngsters, I spent lots of time in my room. It was my quiet place, my sanctuary. I enjoyed being in there with all the things I loved and keeping my space my way.

I always felt comfortable there until, suddenly, I didn't feel comfortable anymore. It would start with a whisper, "maybe that should move over there" or "this just isn't working anymore". And the whisper would get louder until I simply had to listen and make changes to the room. Then I'd be off moving furniture, replacing pictures and re-organizing everything. Sometimes I just changed things around, sometimes I purged things I had outgrown, and organized what was left. Somehow it always felt better after I had taken action. It felt new and fresh: comfortable again.

Back then I wasn't following any system or "rules" of placement. I just moved things around whenever I felt the need for a change, and I kept moving things until they all settled into a new place that felt right. At the time I wasn't aware that I was reacting to unseen energies in my environment when I felt that itch to move things around. In fact, I wasn't aware that my space had an impact on how I was feeling and whether I was thriving or not. I simply listened, moved things, and then usually found some temporary relief in the process.

I'm still not sure whether this need to move things around was in preparation for some change or growth on my part - or a reaction to shifts that had already taken place in my life. Had I evolved as all kids do at a young age and simply realized I needed something new? Or had I subliminally felt that the energy in the space was stuck and that I needed to do something to get it moving so that I could keep evolving?

It wasn't until years later that I stumbled upon *the topic of* Feng Shui *– the ancient art of placement as it's referred to –* and realized that my desire to move things, and my sense of the relief that change brought was no accident. Intrigued by a new knowledge base about how our physical space has a direct impact on our lives, I began to practice it and study it even more.

Armed with a wide range of creative guidelines to follow, I was able to deliberately arrange my space – then my own condo – so that it supported the life/future that I wanted to create for myself.

For more than 10 years now I've been certified as a Practitioner of Feng Shui. I apply Feng Shui in my own home and believe it makes our house more home-ey and welcoming. Feng Shui is the first thing I turn to for every bump in the road, whether it be sudden sleepless nights, financial challenges or simple stuck-ness. I've also been working with clients and am thrilled to be able to use my knowledge of Feng Shui to empower others to harness the energy of their space to create lives and businesses that are rich in every sense.

My intention in writing this book is to empower the reader with an understanding of the impact their space and possessions have on them. I want to show how Feng Shui can be used intuitively for the betterment of their homes and their lives! It's my hope that after reading this book, people will be able to arrange their space with deliberate intention, creating a space that is supportive and energetic, where all occupants can THRIVE!

SECTION ONE

Feng Shui and the Chi of Everything!

Section I – Introduction

In this section, I will introduce you to the basic principles of Feng Shui. You will learn the five elements, the Bagua map, the effects of Chi, where and when to use Feng Shui, and some Feng Shui cures and personal symbols.

1 Inspired Living

What is inspired living?

In my personal and professional experience, inspired living occurs when you approach all areas of your life consciously. Rather than moving through each day reacting to things as they come, you take an empowered and deliberate stance, choosing in advance how you want to be, what you want to do and most importantly how you want it all to feel.

In addition to being deliberate with your life path, you can also consciously arrange your living and workspaces so that they continuously inspire and energize the life you wish to lead. When your living and work spaces are warm, welcoming, easy to move through, and filled with useful and well-loved objects, you will feel safe, comfortable, energized and supported.

A space that is aligned with your dreams and goals and supports you energetically will have a beneficial buzz about it – it may even feel blessed or magical. It will have a good overall vibe that nourishes and energizes you and all that you do. Mindfully creating spaces that feel better and flow better supports all areas of your life, including your health, ability to prosper, ease in relationships and even the way you are seen in the world.

Inspired living includes being somewhere you like to be. When you purposefully set yourself up where your body, mind and soul can feel nourished and supported, you make it easy to perceive and align with your highest aspirations. This is inspired living!

While away from home

Consider how alive and energized you feel when visiting your favorite outdoor landscapes.

You may think of a day by the seaside. You can let your eyes take in the amazing colors of blue sky, white sand, and glistening surf. You can feel the warm sun on your skin and the gritty sand between your toes. You can listen to the rhythmic water lapping at the shore and the sea gulls squawking overhead. You can smell the briny scent of the ocean on the breeze and taste the salt in the air. This natural flow is invigorating.

Maybe a quaint garden is more to your liking? You can notice the pastel beauty and vibrant contrast of the flowers. You can take your shoes off and feel the gravel and grass underfoot. You can stop and smell the roses, of course, and the lilacs, peonies and lavender. You can close your eyes to hear the bees buzz and the birds chirp. You can pick a berry off the vine and taste it for yourself. This natural abundance is calming and uplifting.

Perhaps a thriving cityscape is more your speed. You can spend all day viewing the sprawling architecture and bustling people. You can hear the sound of planes, trains and cars as if it's music to your ears. You can keep your nose busy smelling everything from car exhaust to the street vendor pretzels! You can choose from plenty of foods to taste too. Being a part of it all thrills you. This space is focused and forward-moving.

Everything comes together in these landscapes to awaken each of your senses and make you feel more alive. Your heart-beat steadies, your smiles are quicker, and you feel more at ease when you are where you love to be. Even after a quick trip to one of these thriving landscapes you may return ready to take on the world. If only you could feel like this all the time!

While at home

You visit these places to feel nourished and revitalized. Often, you vacation for a short time, get recharged, and then head home or back to work where you quickly lose that charge and feel depleted again. Why is it that your everyday spaces can't be just as revitalizing to you as these favorite places?

Okay, it may be hard to consistently recreate the kind of energy within your home that your destination escapes have. However, I am here to say that there are many simple adjustments that can sustain energy so that it regularly feels right. Your daily habitats can recharge your batteries rather than deplete them. It is possible to create a space that thrives – a space that is connected, happy, energized and vital.

A better understanding of how dynamically your environment works with your physical body -- either energizing it or depleting it – would probably encourage you to be more particular about the spaces where you spend time and the objects you surround yourself with.

To consider the energy or the "vibe" that colors and objects give off, you simply need to take the time to consider how things make you feel. Does the red paint on the kitchen wall seem a bit too harsh at times? Does that vase on the fireplace mantle make your heart sing when you look at it? Does the desk in the hall that belonged to your Great Aunt feel heavy and burdensome to be the caretaker of? Does the squeaky back door create tenseness and anxiety that lasts long after the noise disperses?

What if you knew that the location of the home you choose, the building itself, the color of the walls, the object on the mantle, your hand-me-down furniture, and the background noises all had an impact on how you were thriving? Would you choose differently?

These things do in fact have a major impact on you, and your ability to thrive! And as a result, they affect all the areas of your life too, including your health, career, relationships, finances, and much more.

If you think about it, this makes perfect sense. When you're feeling good overall then you stay healthier. If you're feeling healthy then you have more energy to put into your career and relationships. In return, your relationships deepen and your finances flow. This works the same with all the other aspects of your life too.

Deliberately setting up your surroundings to support and nourish you creates wellness, and starts life flowing with ease and intention. You begin to benefit in ways you couldn't have before. Your space is feeding your soul, and as a result all areas of your life flow. With a little trust in your own intuition, a general knowledge of how energy works for or against you, and a mindful selection and arrangement of your environment, you can support the important areas of your life for the better!

2 Feng Shui

The ancient art of placement

Feng Shui is referred to as the ancient Chinese art of placement. The goal of Feng Shui is to create harmony and balance in any setting by applying common sense solutions to energetic challenges. The words Feng Shui are translated as wind and water, denoting the importance of the movement and circulation of energy in a setting. Applying Feng Shui within a space can direct the flow of energies to create a clear advantage.

Good fortune

In China it is believed that creating good Feng Shui is a way to cultivate good luck, and direct it to enhance health, wealth and happiness! This is in contrast to the Western view of luck, where getting lucky is considered pure chance, and often outside conscious control. Westerners tend to believe that "You play with whatever hand you're dealt" in life, believing there is not much opportunity to alter your fate. In essence, Feng Shui is an empowering way to alter and enhance your path. By applying Feng Shui principals you can create more ease, and shift outcomes to attract better things into your life. This means more good fortune and more prosperity!

The practice of Feng Shui has evolved from ancient roots in Asia. Feng Shui Practitioners were called in to locate structures so that they would benefit from a healthy flow of "chi" or "source energy" that was already naturally present in the landscape. Ideal sites were safe, protected, fertile, and close to vital resources. Sites with rough terrain, harsh weather, stagnant or rushing water, and/or a lack of wildlife were avoided.

Once a perfect site was located, the Practitioner's next role was to place the structure so that it wouldn't interfere with the natural flow of Chi throughout the area. It was imperative to position the structure without interupting or damaging the physical and energetic surroundings.

Occupants of suitably located buildings would then reap the benefits of the abundant chi. Perhaps their crop harvest would be more successful year after year due to more fertile soils. Or perhaps they simply would be "lucky enough" to avoid harsh weathers and floods that created further challenges.

Ultimately, in China, Feng Shui was used to site everything from homes, palaces, places of business and gravesites. Complete cities were designed according to the basic principles of Feng Shui, with the goal of harnessing the natural forces already present to enhance each structure. Even today, Feng Shui Practitioners are employed to help design modern cityscapes.

In the West, for the most part, planners have not considered Feng Shui when siting structures. Some essential buildings and religious edifices have been placed with care to the direction and surroundings, and some builders may consider sun, wind, and topography when placing constructions. However, most of our homes, businesses, and even whole cities are designed and built with little thought of how they might interrupt the invisible natural energy that is already present.

This omission changes the role that Feng Shui Practitioners play in today's Western world. Practitioners are generally presented with a structure that is already built, likely on less than ideal land, with surrounding fixtures that can't be altered, and with a design and angles that are far from ideal. Here in the West, Feng Shui's benefit is often to heal the damage already done to the land, balance the negative effects of interrupted Chi flow, and redirect and enhance positive energy as much as possible. A positive result of this work is that the energy of buildings is shifted to help support and empower the occupants inside. As you apply the Feng Shui principles presented in this book, you too will most likely be facing the same challenges of working in a space where the inherent flow of energy has not yet been considered. As you'll see, there is still the possibility of improving the space so that it better supports you and all the occupants of the space.

Common practice
It's interesting to note that many ancient cultures have utilized the practice of locating, arranging and designing spaces with energy in mind. Vastu Shastra, Wabi Sabi, Geomancy, the Medicine Wheel, and Feng Shui are various practices that in some way consider the dynamic relationship between people and places. The connection between the surrounding environment and the wellbeing of the occupants is sound practice, not just theory or myth!

Different Feng Shui schools of thought and practice

Over the thousands of years it's been considered, different philosophies have evolved within the practice of Feng Shui. This can cause confusion if you're new to Feng Shui. In effect, modern-day Feng Shui schools of thought can largely be sorted into two fundamental practices: Compass School and Form School. In more recent years, modified versions of these older schools have evolved, including Black Hat Sect Feng Shui and Intuitive/Modern Feng Shui. All of these versions of Feng Shui will get results; some are just more practical to apply in the contemporary western world.

When learning about Feng Shui or hiring a Feng Shui Practitioner, it's important to know the type of Feng Shui being referenced. Some adaptions of Feng Shui use symbols and cures that have culturally specific meaning, while others encourage the use of symbols that resonate with you. Some are based in a system of astrology, some utilize a compass, and others focus on an energy map as tools to redirect natural forces. The key to remember is that all styles of Feng Shui have a variety of useful of resources. Don't let the masses of information and different theories confuse you or hold you back. Whichever adaption of Feng Shui you choose to work with, allow yourself to be empowered to use basic Feng Shui principles -- as well as your own intuition -- to help create a space where you can be your best.

The information presented in this book is based from a Westernized version of Form School Feng Shui. I choose to work with this version because it's less dependent on culturally specific customs, it's easy to understand, and consistently creates positive results. In my own practice, I work with Form School principles first, and call on compasses and other tools if and when they're appropriate.

I have found that a simple mindful connection with your space and what you surround yourself with is what begins to shift the energy in a positive way. Many times that is where I start with clients, layering in enhancements based on the Bagua Map or best directions later.

Ultimately Feng Shui is pretty sensible. You create a clear path for ease in moving through space, you remove items that don't have a clear purpose, and you support goals and intentions through symbolism in the space. Feng Shui helps you take control of your life.

3 Chi

Everything is energy

I often work with clients that are consulting Feng Shui in order to create a space that feels good to be in and sets the client and other occupants up for their best potential. How do we create that "ahhhh" space - a space that feels good and supportive? As you read further, you'll see that many factors are taken into consideration in Feng Shui. One factor is the Chi of the space and how it's flowing. Chi is an invisible vital energy that invigorates all life. It flows through everything. Everything! Chi is present in people, animals, air, water, rocks, buildings, furnishings and even trash! Generally, a space feels good to you when there is positive Chi flowing at a nourishing pace in and around the dwelling.

It's important to define what things and places feel good to you. Can you recall a place you visited recently that had a good vibe? A relaxing spa? A concert with great music playing? A comfortable guest room? Why did it feel so good to you? Was it more energizing than you're used to? Was it more relaxing than your typical day-to-day routine? The colors, the music, the lighting, or the people who were present: all of these have an effect on how the space feels. Each adds an element of energy or Chi to the space that contributes to how you feel there and in effect how you like being there. These places that uplift you with positive emotional atmosphere have good vibrational energy that is flowing in a beneficial way: Good Chi!

It should be noted that not all Chi flow is beneficial. "Sha Chi" typically flows in a direct and/or pointed way at someone or something. The force of this type of flow is too harsh, creating unrest within a space and illness and/or anxiety for the occupants. This flow of Chi needs to be corrected.

> **How do you know if the Chi in your space is healthy Chi that is flowing at a beneficial pace?**
>
> First, notice if you can move easily through your rooms. If you have to move around obstacles or clutter, the Chi is also struggling around those things. On the other hand, if an area is large and wide open with few deflections, this Chi is probably not sticking around very long to nourish the space.

These supportive or detrimental flows of Chi can be witnessed when you pay attention:

In outdoor landscapes, when Chi is obstructed and moves too slowly, it results in adverse effects for the living things around it. Streams stagnate, fields and forests deteriorate, and the people or animals in the area suffer as a result. Likewise, when Chi moves too quickly, it creates problems too. Rivers rage, surrounding land crumbles away, and the landscape is uncomfortable and unsafe for most plant, animal, or human life.

Similarly, every building has an innate life force that arises from the natural Chi that is present on the land, that flows from any Chi that can travel through the space, and that radiates from any objects and people within the space. Ideally Chi moves through an area at a pace that allows it to energize the space within.

Inside a structure, if the Chi moves too slowly, it stagnates and sticks, losing its freshness and ability to nourish a space. Occupants within could feel languid, finances can stall, and relationships may get stale. For example, think of a time when you were in a crowded room and felt like you couldn't catch a breath of fresh air. After a while you'd start to feel hot, anxious, and tired. The flow of Chi has been blocked by the crowd and you physically start to feel the implications of this. This happens subliminally in any space where the Chi is slow or stalling

On the other hand, if the Chi moves too quickly, it cannot energize the space around it and, in effect, it ends up pulling even more Chi away. For example, think about what it is like to stand on the side of a busy road. When a car passes by, the wind pulls at you, almost dragging you over. That same effect happens invisibly in a space when the Chi is moving too quickly. Occupants of the space will feel frazzled and unable to keep up, money can feel like it's going out faster than it's coming in, and relationships may be anxious and tense.

Chi is dynamic and connected

One significant fact about Chi is that it interacts with every object and person as it travels through areas. This interaction can affect the vibration and intensity of the chi. Every object is alive and dynamic, even things we consider inanimate, such as dishware, books, toys, walls (yes, walls!) and furnishings.

The Chi of any object is affected by many different things:

- Is the item mass produced in a factory or lovingly skillfully hand-made by a craftsman?

- Has the item been purchased from a big box store or been gifted lovingly from a friend?

- What color is the object?

- How is it adorned and embellished?

- Has it been well maintained and kept in an honored space or stored in a dusty box?

- What associations are attached to the object by its keeper?

All of this and more have an effect on the Chi of an object and whether that Chi is raising or lowering the Chi of the space around it and the occupants.

The vital life force within any object is actively stored by the piece. The level and quality of this life force Chi can change within the object over time, based on how it's cared for and the energy it encounters from people and other items in the environment.

Have you ever noticed how a child interacts with a favorite stuffed animal or doll? Often they recognize that toy as alive and having personality. After much play and interaction, they create strong attachments with their toys. In addition, groups of toys can create entire storylines of their own. My daughters have grouped toys together into families, or into "good guys" and "bad guys." The Chi of these objects has changed based on the associations the children created about them. Right now some toys are their "best friends" and go everywhere with them. Fast forward ten years from now, and that association will have changed dynamically. Those toys will bring a different kind of energy to my children. Imagine an old, beloved toy of yours that you may have come across as an adult. Can you see how your energy has changed around the toy over time?

Think about some personal possession that you have in your home, a gift from a friend, a framed photo, maybe a stained carpet, or perhaps your aunt's old desk! Notice what thoughts and feelings that piece brings up in you. Notice whether that item is lifting you up and energizing you or weighing you down. You may find that your feelings have changed about an object.

I recently worked with a client who had a beautiful piece of artwork. Initially the painting pleased her because the colors of the artwork complemented her space perfectly, and she recalled buying the piece on a memorable trip she had taken. In the picture a man and a woman each carried a child; it was a happy family of four where each parent carried an equal share of the weight. During our consultation years later, when we talked about the painting, she came to realize that looking at the picture made her sad. Since purchasing it, her marriage had dissolved and her ex-husband had physically and emotionally detached from her and the kids. As a single mother, she carried all of the burden for her family. She no longer had a family of four, and she was carrying all the weight. She felt sad to be reminded of what could have been. After she realized how the energy of this piece was affecting her, and holding her in the past, she decided to give it away.

Other clients had been given a beautiful hand painted vase by a dear friend as a wedding gift; it had a really sweet note from the giver about why they had chosen that particular vase for them. They cherished this vase and put it in a very prominent spot in their home where it could be seen every day. For years it made them happy whenever they looked at it. But a decade later, their relationship with the friend who had gifted the vase had shifted. Their friendship had drifted apart. During our consultation, when they considered the vase more carefully they realized that it had a different association than before: it brought up feelings of sadness and disappointment. It was no longer nourishing them in the way that it used to. It was time let the vase go and let it find a home where it would be loved and cherished again.

I could tell countless stories that clients have shared with me about how various things make them feel. Most of the time they aren't even aware of the energy an object, a sound, or even a scent makes them feel until I repeat it back to them! Recently I had a friend tell me about something in her home that had bothered her tremendously for years. She told me that in the past, when her children were babies, her back door made a wrenching squeaking sound whenever it was used. The noise made her tense up every time she heard it; she'd want to instantly scold "you're going to wake up the babies!" The family lived with this squeaky back door for years even though it created such distress whenever it was used. Finally, when it was fixed, she was thrilled! Of course she wondered why she had put up with the awful noise for so long because now using the door was actually pleasant instead of dreaded.

If you can't change the situation, change your perspective

Sometimes the best fix for something that's irking you about your space is a shift in perception. One client rented an apartment. The carpets were stained and even though she tried cleaning it the spots would come back shortly after cleaning. She felt frustration every time she walked in the door and worse, felt powerless to change it. The landlord wouldn't change the rug, and she couldn't justify the investment herself. We decided to try covering the stains with an area rug and redirecting her focus to something more beautiful inside the entryway. This changed her perception each day when she came home, ultimately shifting the energy around the situation and allowing her to thrive more fully in the space. In this particular case, the client soon moved to a new apartment, leaving that old rug behind. Once you start shifting the energy in the space or the energy around a situation, amazing and unexpected opportunities can come to light!

With practice you can become aware of the Chi that the objects in your environment carry. When you become aware of how the Chi is flowing – or not – within your space, and learn to check in with the personal possessions you keep, you can be empowered to choose and direct the energy so that it's flowing, positive, and supportive.

Chi leaves an imprint

Not only do landscapes, properties, and objects carry Chi that changes over time, spaces and objects also absorb and hold chi. In other words, things that are in a place that has lots of happy activities will absorb lots of happy energy. A spot where arguments abound will have the imprint of anger and negativity. A room where someone has been sick will collect some of that low energy of un-wellness. Have you ever walked into a room and just somehow "felt" that something was off? Maybe you could tell by the looks on others in the room that a disagreement had just occurred. Even though it was over, the energy of it still lingered enough to spark your radar.

You can't hide chi/energy!

It's tempting to think that you can just tuck something away that has not-so-great energy. But unfortunately you just can't hide the Chi or energy of something away. In the example above, hiding was the only option, but be aware that even though it's out of sight, the energy of everything is still connected and interacting with your own personal energy.

Things that we aren't consciously aware of still have an impact on the subconscious level. This works with everything, from the "junk" hidden in the kitchen drawer, to the unfinished project tucked away in the spare bedroom.

Remember that desk inherited from your aunt? It's not really your favorite piece but you feel responsible for it. So perhaps you tuck it away up in the attic so you don't have to look at it and be reminded of the burden it carries. The desk may be hidden, but the unresolved issues of feeling burdened by keeping it or finding a new home for it will not go away!

This has been evident to me on many occasions when I have been with clients and seen the raw emotion an item brings up when they open a closet, or look under a bed and find something they've tucked away to avoid dealing with. One client opened a storage closet and started explaining that this is where she kept all the clothes that fit her before she had her babies. She began to cry as she realized how much energy she had invested into one day being able to fit back into those pieces, and even to one day have that non-mother side of herself back. That closet was full of charged items that reminded her of the person she wasn't anymore! By bringing that stuff back out into the open and going through it she allowed herself to process the unresolved attachments to the clothes from that time period in her life. She had hidden away the clothes and the grief about that part of herself she had lost. Only by taking that stuff out of hiding, and fully acknowledging her feelings was she able to release the contents and the emotion attached to it all.

Why does the energy of stuff matter so much?

We all have items that carry a tremendous amount of energy that is ALWAYS affecting us whether we can see it and choose to pay attention to it, or not. So if everything you own has its own energy that is interacting with your personal wellbeing and the different areas of your life, it's really important for you to be aware of that.

What kind of energy are you bringing into your sacred spaces?

Take some time to check in with the things you surround yourself with and see whether it's feeding you or draining you.

There's a big difference between "yeah, this picture is okay... I thought the size and colors were right anyway" and "OMG, I just love this picture! It reminds me of a trip I took with my family when I was little and we all had so much fun."

If everything that you surround yourself with is chosen to deliberately enliven you and spark excitement, then you will bring that spark with you into all the areas of your life. You can't help but feel better immediately and attract better things and energy to you. Obnoxious noises, stuck windows, clothes that don't fit, old desks, legal papers, clutter and junk, smelly litter boxes, persistent stains and more are all things we may have to put up with from time to time. But be aware that choosing to keep them in your space and not deal with them has an impact on you, your space, your wellbeing and multiple areas of your life. Choose to keep things that feel good, and keep them in a way that uplifts you. Making a conscious and mindful decision about what you own is an incredibly empowering act! Make it a point to check in with your space and possessions regularly and to assess the "vibe" of it all. Is it serving your highest potential? If not move it, or move it on! You'll feel the difference.

4 Principles/Traits of Feng Shui

Yin and Yang

As Chi moves and shifts, it is balancing itself between two extreme forces known as Yin and Yang. Yin energy tends toward feminine, dark, introverted, and restful vibrations. Yang energy tends towards masculine, bright, extroverted and stimulating vibrations. These forces shift and balance in relation to each other. Something cannot be introverted unless taken in context to some level of extroversion. Neither yin, nor yang can exist without the other.

In general, people feel very comfortable in places that have elements of both yin and yang energies. When combined so that neither force dominates, the space feels comfortable and harmonious. However, some spaces should be more of one or the other force based on their function. Spaces that work better when they are slightly yang are living rooms, kitchens and conference rooms. Other rooms are better when the balance of yin energy outweighs the yang energy. This includes spaces where quiet and or concentration are needed, such as bedrooms, libraries or studies.

Years ago, when I was an Event Planner, I remember walking into a huge exhibition hall that was to be the location of one of our events. It was too yang. It had drastically high ceilings, brightly colored walls, vivid lighting, and it was so vast that the slightest noise echoed back and forth. How could we ever convert this into a pleasurable space for a corporate event? The answer was to add some Yin elements to "bring it all down." First carpets were laid for grounding and curtains were used for breaking large areas into smaller more intimate settings.

Overhead lighting was supplemented by accent lighting. Finally, soft seating and linens were brought in to break up the vastness, and background music was added for more soothing white noise. These Yin elements balanced the existing yang elements of the hall and made it a more pleasant venue for the event.

Personal preference lends some weight to deciding this balance too. You may find an open, bright space energizing, so yang energy benefits you. Conversely, your work may require more concentration, so you may thrive better in a quiet, dim, focused space that energetically leans more towards the yin side.

When creating a place that you thrive, it's helpful to know what combination of yin and yang energies speaks to you the most. Consider a favorite place in your home or office, the place where you feel most comfortable and content. Is it more yin or more yang or a balance of both?

The Five Elements

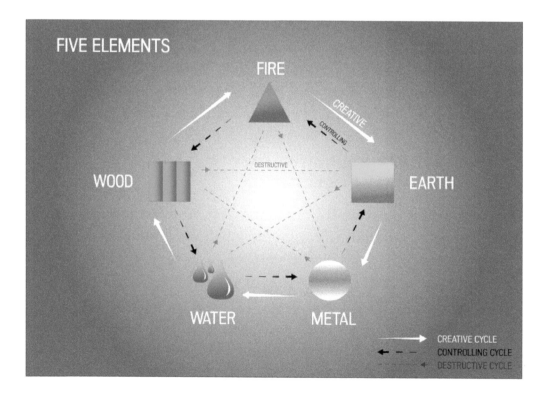

Feng Shui also includes five different elemental compositions when considering chi. Not only do our natural environments carry all five of these elements when balanced, but our human bodies are also comprised of these elements. Because of this fundamental presence, we tend to feel more content and at ease in spaces that contain all of the elements together.

The five elements are Wood, Water, Earth, Metal, and Fire. Each element embodies a different aspect of chi. Bringing all of them into your space can make it feel more balanced, and recover more harmony in your life. It's helpful to understand each element so that you can note its presence or lack of presence in an environment. Too much or too little of any of the elements can have a negative influence on a space. Often you will do everything to make a space look and feel good but it still just doesn't work. This dis-ease with the space is most often due to an imbalance of the elements within it.

Each element has characteristics and associations. There are colors, shapes, materials, locations and directions for each. In addition, elemental groupings can combine to either nurture the energy or to control it in some way.

With practice you can learn to notice the presence of each of the elements and whether they are working with or against each other. A deep understanding of the balance of the five elements is best, but you can start to enhance your own space by noticing how they present themselves around you, and considering how it feels after you add or change objects representing them.

The Wood Element relates to our inner guidance and intuition. Its movement is upward (like a growing tree). It is represented in a space by:

- plants (natural or even silk or artificial ones)

- furnishings made of wood

- images of forests, trees, flowers or greenery

- textiles derived from plant materials

- anything taking the shape of a tree such as columns or stripes

- designs depicting leaves or floral patterns

- colors in the sphere of greens and blues.

When the wood element is excessive within a space, it can create a feeling of overwhelm, impatience and anxiety. When it is deficient in a space, it can be reflected in an inability to begin and cultivate new projects.

The Water Element is associated with our spirit and inner essence. Its movement is naturally downward (like a waterfall). It is represented in an environment by:

- liquids of any type

- structures or furnishings made of glass (including mirrors)

- flowing and curvy shapes

- water features like pools, fountains, wishing wells, lakes or ponds

- images of water and water sources

- darker shades of blue and black

When there is too much water in a space, it can create a feeling of uncertainty and hesitancy in life areas. Occupants can feel overly emotional and weepy. When there is too little water represented, it can result in neediness and lack of concentration.

The Metal Element relates to logic and intelligence. Its natural movement is to go inward or contract (as earth compresses into metal). Metal is represented by:

- Anything made out of precious metals including gold, silver, iron, pewter, copper

- Rocks, gemstones and crystals from the earth (not manmade bricks or pottery)

- Round or oval shapes

- Colors in the white, light or pastel spectrum

- Artwork, statues or sculptures depicting or derived from metal or stone

If the metal element is excessive, it can feel rigid and uncreative. If there is too little metal element present, things can feel disorderly and muddled.

The Earth Element is associated with the body. Its movement is standing ground and connecting (just as the earth is stable and permanent). It is represented in a space by:

- Dirt, mud, potting soil

- Earthenware including tiles, pottery, bricks

- Images of landscapes and dessert settings

- Square and rectangle shapes

- Colors in the sphere of yellows, tans, browns and terra cottas

If the earth element is present to extremes, a space can feel slow, cluttered and stuck. If the earth element is lacking, it can feel flighty and ungrounded.

The Fire Element is reflective of our emotions. Its natural movement is outward (like fiery lava exploding). It is represented by:

- Candles, lights, fireplaces, sunshine

- Anything powered by electricity (televisions, computers, radios, telephones, lights)

- Colors in the spectrum of reds

- Shapes of triangles or pyramids

- Any living being including humans, fish, animals

- Anything made from a living being including leather, fur, or animal-print items

- Artworks depicting light, fire or life

If the fire element is over-represented in a space, it can result in feelings of intensity and turbulence. If there is not enough fire represented in a space, it can feel cold, reserved and unwelcoming.

Play with the elements in your space

Choose a room that you're in often. Pick a tabletop or other surface where you can place some items. Now collect a group of objects — one representing each of the five elements and place them together on the surface. Your collection could include a lamp (fire), a plant (earth and wood) on a round place mat (metal), and a small glass candy dish (water). Each element is represented. Take one of the items away and notice if it seems unbalanced. You may have to play around with items to find things that fit well together, but I am certain you will find that the display looks and feels better — that it simply feels "complete" — when all elements are represented.

One client I worked with recently, had spent much time de-cluttering and organizing her bedroom, yet it still wasn't a place where she desired to be very often. Her room had cool pastel blue walls and white blinds on the window. She did not have any kind of a headboard, just a mattress and pillows that were covered in a pale blue patterned quilt. There was clearly a predominance of metal element and other elements weren't well represented at all. She made two simple changes — finding a wooden headboard and changing the color of the quilt to warmer shades. The colors still accented each other, but they also balanced out the elements of the space and made it feel much more comfortable.

Balancing the elements

The way the different types of Chi interact is a key factor in creating a balanced and nurturing space. When balancing an interior, we are attempting to imitate how these elements interact with each other in nature. There are three different ways that this balance can occur.

First, in the Creative Cycle, elements will support or enhance each other:

Water nourishes wood

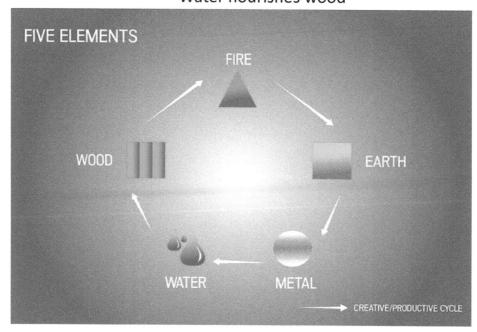

Wood feeds fire

Fire creates earth

Earth compresses into metal

Metal holds water

When one particular element is lacking, you can use its supportive element to strengthen the one that is lacking.

Second, in the Destructive Cycle the elements hinder one another:

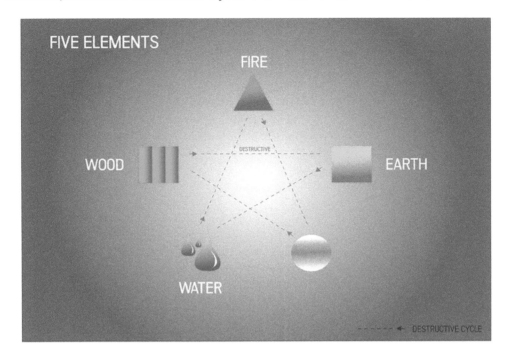

Water extinguishes fire

Fire melts metal

Metal cuts wood

Wood consumes earth

Earth dams water

When one element is overpowering, you can put it in check by adding some of the elements that helps to break down its energy. When fire is out of control, of course, the first thing to do is douse it!

Third, in the Controlling Cycle the five elements weaken each other. This cycle is simply the opposite of the creative cycle:

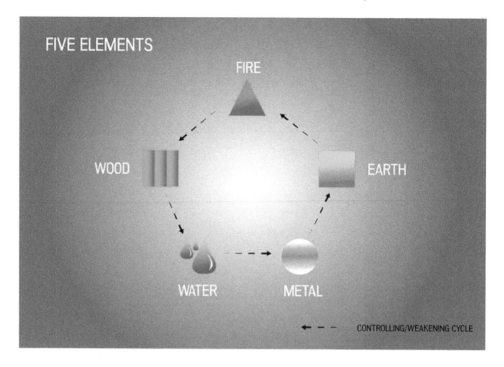

Wood drinks water in order to grow

Fire consumes wood in order to burn

Earth reduces fire by smothering it

Metal weakens earth by transforming its energy into form

Water corrodes metal making it rust

Feng Shui alchemy

The Destructive and Controlling cycles can be used to weaken an element that is present in excess. These cycles are very powerful in Feng Shui to shift the energy of your space. Using the different energies of the elements to balance the space is often called Feng Shui alchemy – it creates an entirely new situation, one that you can thrive in much more effectively.

A bathroom is one room where I often see the need to balance the elements. Bathrooms have many water features including the toilet, faucets, shower heads, and mirrors. A bathroom will feel much more comfortable if all that water is properly balanced with a good mix of the other elements. Wood cabinets, earthy tiles, warm lighting, and colorful towels and curtains can make a big difference in balancing this space out. Think about the difference of walking into a public restroom in a big box store verses walking into a warmly decorated bathroom in a home. It feels very different! Of course bathrooms aren't usually the place that we want to hang out in for long, but we always want to be surrounded by balanced and nourishing energy no matter where we are. Making sure the elements are present and balanced within a room will help accomplish this.

Play with the elements in your space:

Take a brief look around the room you are in. Can you assign each of the items you see into the category of element it most closely represents? Do you notice that there is an abundance of some elements while others are not well represented? Think for a moment about how you usually feel in the space, or how you notice people interacting. Is it stressful, cold, disorganized or hard to concentrate? See if you can notice a correlation between the prominent feeling and which elements are present or lacking.

See if you can move things around so that the room has all of the elements fairly well represented. After a few days, check in and see if you can feel a difference. You can do this throughout your home.

5 The Bagua Map

One of the primary tools used in Form School Feng Shui is called the Bagua Map. It is used to map out land, buildings, homes, and offices to locate the areas that correspond to various life areas such as Health, Love and Money. According to Feng Shui principles, the habitants of these spaces will have more abundance, opportunity and good fortune if the areas are properly mapped out and enhanced with a clear intention of what is wanted from life.

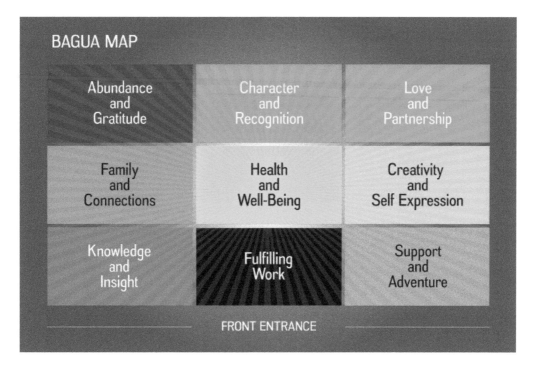

BAGUA MAP

Abundance and Gratitude	Character and Recognition	Love and Partnership
Family and Connections	Health and Well-Being	Creativity and Self Expression
Knowledge and Insight	Fulfilling Work	Support and Adventure

FRONT ENTRANCE

The Bagua Map is a simple square or rectangle that is divided equally into 9 sections referred to as guas. Each gua relates to one of the nine life areas: Fulfilling Work, Support and Adventure, Creativity and

Self Expression, Love and Partnership, Character and Recognition, Abundance and Gratitude, Family and Community, and Knowledge and Insight. By applying the Bagua Map over our homes, we can see that all sections of the space we occupy have substantial meaning, as do all parts of our life.

You can get a glimpse into what is going on in your life based on what's going on in each of these areas of your space. Once you have mapped out your living space or work space you can take a closer look at each area and see if there are any symptoms of dis-ease. You may discover clutter building up in some spaces that corresponds to a life area you struggle with. You may notice that the embellishments you have chosen to decorate with are contradictory to what you want for a specific life area. There's no limit to what you might discover!

Using the Bagua Map to locate the various life areas within your home is a simple yet powerful way to effect different results for your life. When you identify a life area that you want to work on within your space, you can balance the energy and add meaningful enhancements to create amazing shifts in that area.

Before we learn how to apply the map to our homes, let's first learn about each of the Guas, what they mean, and how they impact us. We'll start from the front and center Gua of the map, the Fulfilling Work Gua, then follow it around counter clockwise, ending in the center of the map:

Fulfilling Work

Starting front and center of the Bagua Map is the Fulfilling Work Gua. This is the area that is related to your chosen profession. It is the space that holds the energy of your passion! It is associated with the work you do, and the way that you put yourself out into the world. Ideally, your work is so fulfilling that you would do it even for free. Focus on this area of your space if you are facing challenges at work, you are unhappy with your career path, or you are looking for work.

Support and Adventure

Moving to the front right of the Bagua Map is the Support and Adventure Gua. This area is about the helpful people and freedom that you have in your life. Are you well supported in life? Do you have family, friends, colleagues and neighbors that you feel you can reach out to when you get into a jam? This area is associated with the concept of synchronicity or being in the right place at the right time. If you are well supported, you have more freedom to move about and be in the flow of life, making the right connections in the right places. When this area is in order, the puzzle pieces of life fall into place effortlessly and great things to come your way. Focus on this space when you need support in a particular area, have a trip planned, or would like to do more travel.

Creativity and Self Expression

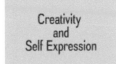

In the right middle of the map is the Creativity and Self Expression Gua. This area is about the pleasure that comes from creative expression. This area is associated with the playful inner child, the creative artistic process and the creative process of bearing children.The children, artwork, music and other creative endeavors that derive from this area bring joy to us and the world around us. It is a magical reciprocal gift. This is the Gua to look at when you are embarking on a creative project, seeking more joy in your life, or wanting to have children.

Love and Partnership

The far right corner of the Bagua Map is the Love and Partnership Gua. This area supports your relationship to yourself and to your partner. It is associated with all relationships, whether it's a romantic or business connection. Ideally, relationships are supportive, built on trust, and balanced so that each partner can thrive. If you are single, this area reflects your relationship with yourself and how you love yourself. Do you nurture yourself as needed and give yourself permission to allow whatever your true needs are? As the saying goes, you need to love yourself first before someone else can love you. This is the corner to focus on when you want to attract a new relationship, improve your current partnership, or focus on developing your relationship with yourself.

Character and Recognition

The far middle section of the Bagua Maps relates to the Character and Recognition Gua. This area is about the moral fiber we present to the world and how we are recognized. It reflects the relationship we have with the community and networks around you as well as the legacy you will leave behind. What contribution do you want to make? How do you want to be seen by others? What do you want to be known for? It is important to be mindful of how you are perceived, because this is something you will carry with you for a very long time. A good reputation will open doors for you, while a bad reputation will be hard to shake. Focus on this Gua if you want compensation or recognition for your work, if you want to create a good standing in the community, or if you want to be well known for something.

Abundance and Gratitude

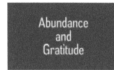

The Abundance and Gratitude Gua is in the far left corner of the Bagua Map. This area is about money and finances, but also about other forms of wealth, including the things that money can't buy. It's important to recognize richness in all of its forms. For example, when your wallet feels light, can you find evidence of plenty elsewhere, like noticing your full tank of gas, food on the table, or good health? These are all things that are of great, if not more, value than actual cash flow. Having gratitude plays a large role in creating abundance. Another concept that is critical regarding wealth is that of having trust. This area supports knowing that you have enough of everything and trusting that you always will. It is about believing that the universe provides all that you need and being open to receiving all it has to offer. This is the Gua to focus on if you want to generate more cash flow in your life, or if you would like to be more aware of the abundance that surrounds you daily.

Family and Connections

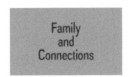

The Family and Connections Gua is located in the middle left section of the Bagua Map. This area supports the relationships we have with our family, ancestors, and even our family at work. A strong connection with our family is like a strong root system that holds us in place. Family has our back and encourages us so that we can grow tall. We can lean on our extended family when life gets bumpy. We benefit from the support and opportunity that those unconditional relationships offer. This is an area to focus on when you want to strengthen and honor family ties, when you want to heal severed family relationships, or when you want to work through a family scandal or shame.

Knowledge and Insight

The Knowledge and Insight Gua is the front left section of the Bagua Map. This space supports our thirst to grow intellectually and spiritually. It also supports the desire we have to find out who we are on the inside. This is about connecting with our soul desires and our innate intuition. Do you give yourself the time and space to pursue all of your interests? Do you give yourself the opportunity to continue growing and learning about yourself and the world around you? Do you allow yourself to connect to your inner knowing and that of any unseen guides that you have? Do you allow yourself both time and space to be quiet, reflect and listen? This is the area to focus on for school and study of any kind, especially during crunch times like tests or finals. Be aware of this Gua if you have a special interest to pursue, want to create a more mindful lifestyle, or want to connect more easily to your own intuition or universal guidance.

Health and Well-being

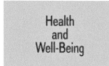

The center Gua of the Bagua Map is related to Health and Well-being. It is the quiet place surrounded by life. It is still, like the eye of a storm, while the other life areas move and flow around it. Ideally the center of ourselves and our homes is a grounded and peaceful place that helps support the rest of life's treasures. This area is a reflection of how we're taking care of ourselves. When our health and well-being are good we're able to be available for all that life has to offer. When they are suffering we tend to miss out on things and other areas of life can quickly suffer too. Focus on this Gua to help ground and center all of the life areas and to create balance and vitality for yourself and your home.

Use this box to sketch your floor plan

How to use the Bagua Map

Applying the Bagua Map to the space you are working on is easy! Some people are simply able to visualize or imagine a structure divided into the Bagua Map's nine quadrants without needing to draw it out. For most, it's easiest to start by sketching the layout of the building you're working with as seen from above it. In other words, draw a bird's eye view of the space, as accurately and to scale as possible. Be sure to include all areas that are under the roof line, including covered porches, additions, bumped out entryways and attached garages. If the building is made up of multiple floors, complete a layout for each floor on a separate piece of paper.

Next, lay tracing paper over the floor plan and draw the nine quadrants of the Bagua Map over the layout. The whole house should fall within the border of the Bagua Map you have drawn, so the Bagua Map may stretch to become a longer or wider rectangle as needed to cover the whole structure. (If your home is not a square or rectangle, you will have some empty spaces falling within your Bagua Map. We'll address this shortly.) Next, line up the front of the map, so that it corresponds with the architectural front entrance to your home. (The front of the map is always the side where the Knowledge and Insight, Fulfilling Work and Support and Adventure Guas lie.) The architectural front door is the door that would have been intended to be used as the main entrance as it was built, but may not be the door you currently use most often.

If the main door is in the front center of the house, you are entering the Fulfilling Work section of the home. If the door is on the front, right of your home, you are entering your home through the Support and Adventure section. If your door is on the front left side of your home, you are entering through the Wisdom section. In all three cases the Abundance section will be the far left corner of your structure and the Love and Partnership area will be in the far right corner of your space.

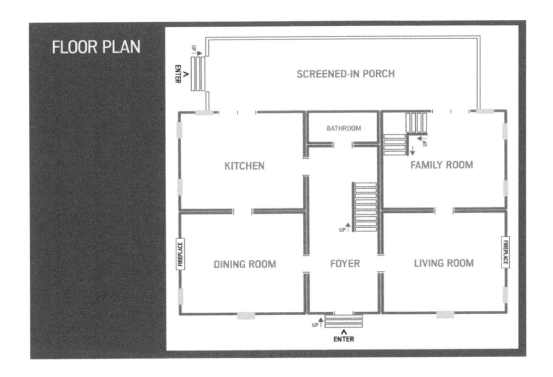

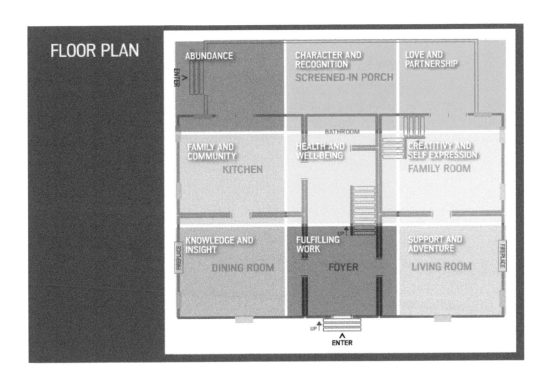

Missing areas

If your home is not a perfect square or rectangle, you will likely be "missing" areas. When some of the life areas of the Bagua Map fall outside of your roofline and structure, these are considered missing areas. For example, all or part of the Love and Partnership gua may be absent in an L-shaped home. Character and Recognition is most likely missing in a U-shaped home. The diagrams show a home where all of the Fulfilling Work and Knowledge and Inspiration areas, and part of the Well-being and Family areas, are not represented in the structure.

If part of the Bagua Map is absent from your home, consider if the missing Life Areas are also deficient, or hindered in your life. Once you are aware of the challenges provided by your space you can remedy it within the space, often alleviating or lessening the existing trials you've been facing or may encounter.

The Fix

If you discover that you have a missing area, there are several things you can do. First, assess the space and consider if and how it's being reflected in your life. Are you missing part of the Abundance corner and feeling like you can never gather enough wealth? Perhaps the Support Gua falls outside of your house. Do you also feel like you can't find helpful people that you need easily? Notice if things are manifesting in your life in ways that are related to the unrepresented area. Even if you don't see a relationship, it's still important to make corrections to your space. In most cases the fixes are easy. I consider it preventative medicine – well worth the time and investment.

Next, after you've assessed things, see if you can find a way to create a foundation for the missing area. Consider where the walls of the Gua would be and where they would intersect outside of your current structure. Place something significant and symbolic where that intersection would be. You could bury a crystal in the ground, place a rock at the intersection, plant a tree, or position a post with

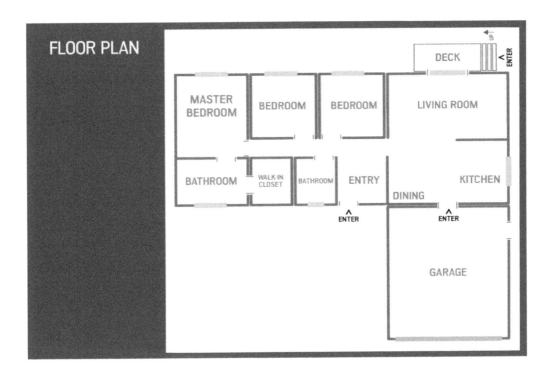

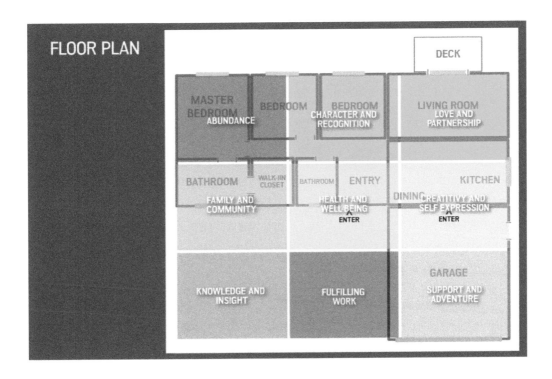

bird feeders coming off of it in the corner. You could even fence in the missing area and create an outdoor room. Ideally, if you have a Life Area that falls outside of your structure, you can clean up the area, beautify it in some way, and make it as useful as possible. This will ground and hold the energy needed to sustain this space of the home.

Finally, you can further correct the energy of the missing area by locating that Gua in each one of your rooms, and placing an appropriate enhancement in that space. For example, if you were missing the Abundance corner of your house, you could find the Abundance corners in the bedrooms, living room, dining room and kitchen, and enhance that corner in each room. This can be done by making sure those corners are clutter free, useful, and by adding some symbol that reminds you of the feeling of wealth and abundance that you want to have.

Don't give up!

Many people get to this part of applying the Bagua Map to their space and then become immediately disheartened by what they discover. They look at their findings and think "Oh great, I don't even have an Abundance area!" or "if I'm missing the Love area then there's no way I'll ever find the relationship I want." Instead, I encourage you to look at your findings as "knowledge is power." Contrary to some misconceptions, there are simply no challenges that can't be alleviated or completely fixed with Feng Shui. Even the dreaded missing area can be rectified! Not being aware of it, or simply ignoring the problem once it's identified is NOT the right thing to do! Be empowered with what you find out about your space. It's all good, so keep going!

There are many ways to use the Bagua Map of your home to identify challenges and/or improve the flow of the space. In my own home I use the Bagua Map to identify my challenge areas. I often notice that clutter collects in the same Gua area of each room. Usually it's just inside the doorway, often coinciding with the Career sector. As an entrepreneur, I'm often juggling many roles at once, and it can be ineffective. It's clear from looking at the sticking points in each Gua of our Bagua Map that this is the area of life that presents the most challenges for me.

Other ways to use the Bagua Map:

Now that you know how to correct for any missing areas, consider the other ways to analyze your space using the map. Take a look through your house with the Bagua Map in mind and notice what symptoms of dis-ease you see. Be mindful of where the broken furniture is, notice where the piles of clutter tend to collect within your space, and finally, pay attention to where challenging features, like bathrooms and laundry rooms, fall within the Bagua. Assessing your home through the eyes of the Bagua can shed a lot of light on the challenges that you face in each area of your house, as well as the challenges presented in life itself.

In one of my client's cases, a home was missing large parts of the Abundance Corner and the Love and Partnership Corner due to an addition in the back of the house. We used the Bagua Map to determine where the corner of the foundation of each of these guas should have been. The client then buried two large crystals in the ground at these corners to symbolically re-build these areas. She also placed appropriate accent pieces in those outdoor spaces including a romantic bench where she and her partner could sit in the Love corner, and a fountain in the Abundance corner as a symbol of flowing money. We then used the Bagua Map to locate the Abundance and Love Corners in each interior room of the house.

The client placed enhancements that would further ground and energize these corners. After these cures were in place she reported that both of these life areas felt very secure to her.

Now that you know how to apply the Bagua Map to a space, keep in mind that you can apply it pretty much everywhere! You can apply the Bagua Map to an entire city, a single piece of property, an individual building, one particular room in a space, or even on any flat surface like a desk. You can even use all these layers of Bagua Maps to completely enhance every aspect of the space: One map for the entire property, another for the entire house, a map for each floor, and then a map over each room! This technique of layering comes in very handy when you have a specific area of interest that you want to bring extra energy to.

Bagua Map verses primary room function:

In addition to mapping space according to the Bagua Map, you can also consider the primary purpose of each room and how it is related to one of the life areas. For example, bedrooms are clearly related to Love and Relationships, even if the bedroom does not fall in the love Gua. Home offices are strongly related to your career, even if they don't fall in the Fulfilling Work Gua.

So in addition to mapping out your space according to the Bagua Map and adding enhancements and cures based on what you find, you can also enhance each room based on what its primary purpose is. This, done in addition to applying the Bagua Map, adds an extra layer of clarity and symbolism to your space that is very powerful.

Even if your bedroom falls in the Abundance corner, you can still make it a lush and romantic retreat, while at the same time choosing fabrics, décor and colors that feel rich and abundant and symbolize wealth to you. And if your home office falls in the Family and Community Area, you can bring in images and symbols of a strong family unit while also enhancing it with strong symbols that keep you focused in your career endeavors.

When you arrange and adorn a space based on both its primary purpose *and* the Bagua Map, you'll be considering your space even more deliberately and energy will flow to those life areas respectively.

Which Gua for litterboxes, trash and other unpleasantries:

What if you have all the areas but notice that you have some unpleasant things located in some of the Guas? Perhaps your Love Gua is the only place you can keep your litter box, your Health and Well-being Gua is where the bathroom is, or your trash cans have to remain staged in the Character and Recognition Area.

Again, awareness is the key. Sometimes you just can't relocate the stuff or activity that's taking place in key areas. Of course it would be ideal to have a vibrant solarium with plants in the Health Gua, and a romantic bedroom in the Love Gua. But that isn't always possible, especially when we're working with structures that were built and defined without considering Feng Shui.

If the area can't be used in its ideal way, at least keep it clean, functional, enhance it as you can, and then be sure to enhance the challenged Gua in all the other rooms of your space. So keep the litter box in your love corner if you need to, but keep it clean, hang a picture of a pair of loving cats near it, and then go and enhance the love corner of all your other rooms to make up for it!

Apartment dwellers can use the Bagua too:

If you live in an apartment that is part of a larger building housing other residences, you can still apply the Bagua map. First, place the map over the entire building and determine which gua or guas your designated living space falls into. Second, map out your apartment individually and lay the Bagua over it from the main entrance to your apartment. You may find that some of your Life Areas fall into apartment spaces that are occupied by neighbors. Although challenging, you can still address it easily by placing cures for the missing spaces in the correct sections of individual rooms.

6 When to Use Feng Shui

Feng Shui is a tool that can be used simply to make a space feel more peaceful and comfortable, but as you know by now it can also be a much more powerful tool to shift energy, to support life changes or ease the bumps of challenging circumstances. Generally, any significant change in status -- new job, job loss, new partner, divorce, new house, new life goal, or even being stuck-- is benefitted by the use of Feng Shui.

Feng Shui is my go-to tool for any situation. When my children have trouble sleeping I look at what's going on with the Feng Shui in their bedrooms. When financial stress hits, we move furniture! When I'm looking for more Feng Shui Practitioner opportunities or my husband is going for career advancement, we sweep out old energy and call in new blessings. We constantly re-evaluate our space based on what we aspire to create. Whenever I enter into a situation where I am unsure or lacking clarity, I automatically start cleaning and clearing my space. Feng Shui has never disappointed me.

Here is just a small list of situations where you can apply Feng Shui to bring about positive change.

Career opportunity: Perhaps you simply want more recognition at work. Maybe you are seeking a promotion or applying for a new job entirely. You could be venturing out on a new business enterprise, or looking to attract more clients to your current business. Perhaps you are seeking clarity about what your passion is and what will bring you the most fulfilling work. Feng Shui is the perfect empowering tool for all of these challenges.

To find clarity: Perhaps you are immersed in a situation and you can't see a clear resolution. Or maybe you have a question that needs answering. Or perhaps you don't see what the next clear step is on your current path. In these situations, when clarity isn't coming easily, taking some time to shift the energy in your space can bring incredible lucidity to a situation.

To make a change in a relationship: You may suddenly realize that your current relationship needs to be rescued; you may be single and seeking to attract a partner; or you may have just ended a relationship and are looking for closure and clarity. Maybe you realize that you are immersed in a pattern of attracting the wrong partner or being unable to keep a partner. Perhaps you are in business and seeking to ease relations with current partners or to attract the best new partners. Using the environment to support the energy of partnerships is a very powerful use of Feng Shui. When you are ready to shift the energy around your relationship past, shifting the energy of your space will provide tremendous support.

To be viewed differently in the world: Maybe you're looking to change people's perception about you or the work you do, you want to be recognized for something different, you're stepping into a new role that you want credibility in, or you simply wish to establish a legacy for which you'll be remembered. Feng Shui is a great way to illuminate the vision you have for yourself in the world.

To meet financial challenges: Perhaps you receive an unexpected bill or sudden change in income that causes financial stress and tightness for you, your family and/or your business. You notice that cash flow always seems inconsistent, coming in fast sometimes, but never having enough at the right time. Maybe it simply feels like money is always going out or faster than you can ensure it comes in. You may be ready to shift some old patterns around lack, guilt about money, difficulty receiving, letting go, or recognizing and being grateful for current abundance. Cash flow is Chi flow. So when you use Feng Shui to get the Chi moving in a beneficial way through your space you will eventually see an ease in financial tensions.

To strengthen ties with family, friends, coworkers: Let's face it, sometimes relationships get strained. Whether tensions lie with someone you share the household with, someone you share office space with, or someone across the miles, you can use Feng Shui to call attention to and energize the connection. Sometimes people just give up, especially when the link has been broken for years. Family, friends, and co-workers are part of our foundation in life, so creating and supporting good bonds with them goes a long way in creating ease through the rest of our lives. Feng Shui is an effective way to support the positive parts of the relationship and create a place for healing and reconciliation.

To study or enhance learning: If you're embarking on a new area of study, heading off to college, or preparing for a test, you can use Feng Shui to direct the energies in your favor as you set forth. From directing the Chi flow so that it supports your focus to emphasizing your goals to keep you inspired, there are many benefits to enhancing a study space to energize it and support your academic progress.

To start a business: I can't emphasize enough how helpful and supportive Feng Shui can be when you are starting a new endeavor. Whether your new business will be run from your car, your home, a new office space, or a retail establishment, Feng Shui should always be considered. Feng Shui takes into account your overall vision, your business goals, your professional relationships, the attractiveness of your establishment and much, much more. When Feng Shui has been used, clients will see you more favorably, you'll see yourself and your vision better, and the energy will positively flow around your new enterprise. Deliberately designing your business plan and physical space according to Feng Shui philosophy will set you and your venture up for success.

To buy or sell a house: If you are getting ready sell your home, or you're in the market for a new home, Feng Shui is a powerful tool to consider. When selling a property, it's important to alleviate any Chi flow challenges to help the space look and feel attractive to potential buyers. Houses hold energy, and it's especially effective to clear negative energies and break energetic ties so the home is easy to release and then easily attracts and appeals to new buyers.

If you're seeking a new home, consult Feng Shui to identify Chi challenges and make sure they can effectively be cured so the new home fully supports you and all occupants. Just last week I received a call from a former client who put an offer on a house. She called me the day after the deal was done to let me know about it and line me up for a consultation as they get ready to take ownership of the new space! When you've made such a large investment in your home it's worth it to protect and enhance it with proper Feng Shui!

To recover following prolonged illness or death in the home: Both illness and death leave an energy imprint within a space. If an occupant of the home has been unwell or if anyone in the house has passed on, it's important to clear away the residual energies and invite in fresh and healing energies. It's also helpful to look at the Chi flow and make sure it is arranged to encourage health and wellbeing for everyone else in the home and support family members who have been through the challenges. Feng Shui is a wonderful tool that encourages vital life flow. It's especially helpful to shift things around and look at things from a fresh perspective after being held for a long time by illness or grief.

To encourage health: When energy is not flowing in a space, the occupants will suffer from that deficiency of proper Chi flow. This can manifest as illness, exhaustion, nervousness, depression, infertility, or a simple lack of wellbeing. Feng Shui can be used to alter and direct the Chi flow, encouraging health, vitality, a place to rest and recuperate, and ultimately supporting a healthier body, mind and spirit.

To support a new goal: Whether your seeking Olympic gold, setting new health and weight goals, or striving for your degree, Feng Shui encourages the attainment of goals by supporting your path with clear symbols and vital energy. In addition to avid training, consistent concentration and whatever other tools you use, Feng Shui can encourage and support you during each step toward hitting your target.

To get unstuck: Creative blocks are a sign of energy that is not flowing through you. Finding ways to release the energy flow in a space will ultimately trickle down to energy for the occupants of the space too. If you're an artist who is creatively blocked, someone who is looking to start a family, or an adult simply wishing to encourage more childlike playfulness in areas of your life, Feng Shui can increase and alter the stream of creative energy.

Where can you use Feng Shui?

Feng Shui can be applied *anywhere.* Feng Shui cures and enhancements can be applied to any flat surface in a space ... to any room in question ... to any home, business or building ... to any outbuilding such as a shed, barn or garage ... to any yard, landscape or outdoor property!

Feng Shui can also be applied on a much larger scale to a neighborhood, community, campus or city block. Zoom out and it can also be applied to any town or city to make adjustments. Feng Shui can be powerfully layered on each of these segments of your world to positively align energies in your favor. Remember that in ancient China, Feng Shui was applied to ancient temples and whole cities.

7 Feng Shui Cures and Personal Symbols

Feng Shui Cures

When working with Feng Shui, you'll often hear the term "Feng Shui cure" or "Feng Shui remedy." These refer to various methods that are applied to help shift the energy of the space as well as to specific objects that are placed with intention to alter or move the energy throughout the space.

Feng Shui cures work in various ways. Some actually shift and change the energy within the space. In this case, adding something that has a higher or lower vibration to the space, such as a specific color, sound, scent or object can raise or lower the more vibration and shift the feel of the room. Other cures work by helping to focus your intentions on your goal. For example, when you're studying for a big test it would be helpful to place post- it notes throughout your space with A+ written on them. These cures help you succeed through the power of suggestion; the remedy becomes a mental aid in getting you where you want to go.

Feng Shui cures can assist in shifting the energy in various ways. Some cures, such as moving furniture or clearing clutter help to unblock energy. Other cures are activating, helping to raise or redirect the flow of chi. Remedies such as wind chimes, fans, mirrors, crystals help in this instance. Cures like statues, rocks and heavy furniture create a different cure by helping to stabilize and ground a space.

Here are examples of traditional Chi enhancers:

Wind chimes

Wind chimes are a vibrant enhancement. They lift and shift the energy by adding vibrational sound and movement to a space. They can be made of various materials including metals, shells, and wood so they can often be used to balance the elements of a space. For the best effect, choose a set of chimes that has the most pleasing tone.

© Laurie Mounce

Water features

This includes water fountains, ponds, aquariums and more. Adding any reminder from nature is a powerful cure for a space but water is particularly powerful because it adds motion, flow and sound as well. As mentioned before, in Feng Shui, water is also considered a strong symbol for money. Adding it to any space can be a cure to encourage a positive flow of money! When placing a water feature, direct the water flow towards the interior of the home so that the current sends energy in the direction that more Chi is desired.

Natural Crystals

© Kerri Miller

Crystals and gemstones mined from the earth help to ground and balance a space. Different types of crystals have specific characteristics so you can match the type of crystal to the effect you desire to enhance in your space. For example, rose quartz is traditionally used to attract romance, while citrine is often placed as a symbol of wealth. Working with crystal energy in Feng Shui has amazing potential.

Faceted Crystals

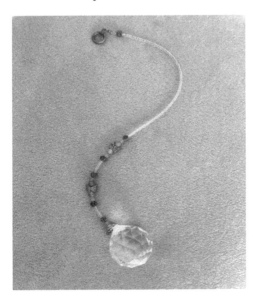

© Kerri Miller

These are clear crystals that are cut causing light to refract through them. These shift the energy of the space by lifting and circulating the light rays (aka chi) as it comes into a space. Faceted crystals can be found in many shapes and sizes, but generally round spheres are preferred for Feng Shui uses. Crystals can be hung in the center of a room to lift and circulate chi, or in a window to redirect chi.

Color

Colors are one of the simplest Feng Shui cures for a space. Every color has its own vibration so a new color changes the vibe of a space immediately. A simple shift in color can alter the energy by making a space warmer or cooler. Adding color and/or patterns can easily move a space from more yin to more yang. Colors are an easy way to bring the various elements into a space, as each element is represented by a color. Of course color has been proven to elicit specific moods and emotions in the occupants of a space:

Some meanings of various colors:

Red – encourages self-expression

Blue – builds self-esteem and encourages calm

Green – encourages growth and expansion

Yellow – promotes cheerfulness

Orange – promotes creativity and cooperation

Purple – symbolizes wealth and spirituality

Pink – encourages romance and connections.

White – symbolizes new beginnings and purity

Living things

Fish, animals, plants and people all add energy to a space. Need to add a little energy and excitement to a space? Any living thing will do that. Think of how a puppy bounding into a room immediately shifts the vibe that's going on. Or consider how a sleeping cat can signal comfort and calm in a room. Living things are Chi in motion – natural energy shifters. You can up the energy of a quiet space simply by bringing in symbols of living things too. If you're not an animal lover, or don't have a room of people to call on, you can still represent that kind of active energy in your space with symbols of them. Consider animal prints in your décor or whimsical statues of children as a cure for adding life, spark and energy to your space.

Plants

Like water, adding potted plants to a space is a simple way to bring some living nature into your space. They represent the wood element and encourage growth, upward energy and expansion. Their natural ability to purify air makes them a strong symbol of healthy living. Plants and flowers are also a strong symbol of abundance. If taking care of live plants is not an option in a space, silk plants, or even artwork that depicts plants and greenery can be substituted. Although real flora will bring the highest energy to a space, the energy of these substitutes will surely be stronger than that of a dying plant!

© Kerri Miller

The effects of a picture or silks house plants will be subtler than the real thing, but still positive all the same. Whether your plants are real or not, be sure to take good care of them. The more love you give them they more love they will add to your space.

Sound

Sound is vibration and changing the vibration in a space changes the energy. Sound is a great cure, especially for breaking up stagnant energy or changing the mood. Consider music, laughter, chirping birds, wind chimes and more to cure the space. If you're used to listening to talk radio or usually have a television on in the background, consider changing the station or choosing a different artist to play to alter the energy around you and ultimately shift your mood as needed.

Mirrors

Mirrors are powerful cures to be used in a space. They can be used to absorb energy, reflect it, double the energy of something, or even to expand a view. Because of this multitude of possible reactions that mirrors can create within a space, it's always important to place a mirror with awareness and intention for what you want it to do. Once a mirror is placed, watch for results and notice how the energy shifts. You may need to correct the placement if you notice unintended results.

Make sure that mirrors reflect something pleasant to look at. We certainly don't want to reflect and symbolically double the energy of something unpleasant. Mirrors are also a potent symbol of self-awareness, so make sure that mirrors are hung in a way that all dwellers can see a complete and clear reflection of themselves. It can be disconcerting day after day to walk by a mirror that only shows part of you, or that distorts your image as you peer into it. Finally, care should always be taken when placing mirrors in the bedroom. If poorly placed, they can move the energy in ways that are unsupportive of sleep and well-being.

Scents

Scent is a powerful way to not only shift energy, but to instantly change your mood and feelings. Each scent has a unique energetic vibration, just like music and colors, so when you add a scent to your space you're changing the vibration of the space. You can use different aromas effectively to add or reduce energy and the occupants in the spaceit alters will react similarly. Marketers have known this power for years and often use scent in shopping centers, hotel lobbies, etc. to create a sense of ease and encourage people to stay longer. There is a huge difference between chemically created scents like fragrances and perfumes, and pure scents drawn from aromatic plants. Although manufactured scents can elicit a response, it's a different energy entirely that you're inviting into your space. I think of it the same way I think of real verses silk plants. The silk plants can be aesthetically pleasing and balance the elements in a room, but they lack the benefits of adding energetic life and even literal oxygen to the room.

Some of my favorite oils to shift a space include the following:

- Uplifting a Space – citrus oils like Lemon, Grapefruit or Orange

- Calm a Space – Lavender or Chamomile

- Encourage focus or study – Peppermint or Rosemary

- Encourage romance – ylang ylang or rose

- For grounding and meditation – sandalwood, patchouli

There are a number of ways to diffuse the oils into the space: burn a candle that is scented with the pure oils, put a few drops of oil into a spray bottle with water and then spray it through a space, diffuse the oils through a room with an electric diffuser, or drop essential oils into a steaming pan of water and let the steam carry the scent. Honestly, adding a pleasing scent to a space is one of the fastest ways to shift the energy and literally get into the head of the occupants to shift their energy too!

Lights and Candlelight

Lighting can instantly add or change the energy of any space. Place a lamp in a dark room and it suddenly feels uplifted. Position accent lighting around a too bright room and the vibe is toned down. Lighting is a great way to shift the mood of any space, especially by using a variety of lighting options including uplights, stringlights, candles and more. To call energy to any Life Area, add light.

Images, words, and punctuation

Deliberately choosing artwork, and décor that sets the tone you are trying to create for your life is a very powerful Feng Shui cure. When you're looking to eat healthier, you can place images of healthy, freshly prepared foods in your kitchen sightline. Lately, there's a trend for using artwork depicting words or quotes that inspire ways of living within a space. The key here is consciously choosing accents that support your goals, rather than filling you walls and shelves with space savers that mimic magazine pictures. Choose artwork that appeals to you and place it thoughtfully throughout your residence as a cure and enhancement to how you want to be reminded to live.

Personal Objects that Elicit Emotion for you

It's very powerful to choose your own cure for a Feng Shui challenge. I always encourage using items that make you feel most comfortable and that intuitively speak to you as a remedy in the space. Any personal object that makes you feel good or represents a certain feeling you want to create in that life area is appropriate to use as a Feng Shui cure or remedy.

You can use personal items in a few different ways. First, you can simply add items that make you feel good – lift your thoughts and your mood and the mood/ vibration of your space will change. Second, you can consider what type of remedy you need for each situation. Here are some examples of this method:

For someone looking to inspire more creative work

Consider highlighting pieces or accents in the space that stimulate a flow of fresh ideas. For some that might simply mean creating a space where creativity can happen – with a pen and notebook or blank canvas and art supplies at the ready. Others might be inspired by filling a space with idea books, stimulating images, or sample works to try. With one client that had a creative studio, we created an inspiration wall where she could display idea books, patterns to try, and inspiring work by other artists.

For someone looking for a loving relationship in their life:

Consider what things feel romantic and symbolize an equal partnership? One person might want to hang love poems on the wall while another might like symbols of pairs like a vase with two flowers in it. Clarity is a factor here! It goes a long way to simply create a list of attributes you would like to find in a romantic partner. Of course this would be different for everyone.

Simply consider what your challenge is and what things you can add or highlight in your space that intuitively provides support and encouragement in shifting the energy around. Also remember to keep it simple. A few things that feel *great* are better than a bunch of things that feel okay! Keep being aware of the energy of the things you're surrounding yourself with.

For someone noticing financial distress

Consider the things that make you feel rich and abundant. For some adding thick silky fabrics and jewel toned accents to a room might be encouraging and attracting of more abundance. For others it may be pictures from a lavish trip they have taken or would like to take. It's especially powerful to look for natural abundance around you and capitalize on it. Every few years our trees drop an immense number of pine cones so I gather them up into baskets and use them as arrangements on our front steps, deck, and through the yard! It's a great reminder to me of the richness that can be found when you look for it.

Personal Patterns

What are the things you surround yourself with saying about you? What do the things that surround you mean to you??

One of the reasons that changing, and moving things around in your space, is beneficial is because in the process you break up old and unsupportive patterns. Subconsciously we choose spaces that match our inner comfort zone. In Feng Shui terms, our outer environment is a direct expression of what's going on inside of us. Our homes outwardly mirror our internal, emotional states. To the trained eye your space reveals a great deal about you. Where ever you're stuck in your head is probably showing up in your space, affecting areas of your life and continuing to hold you back.

I've seen this represented in so many ways.

- Single women drawn to artwork that highlights a lone woman in the image.

- Unapproachable Business Managers who have obstacles placed throughout their office

- A person spread too thin amongst many obligations, whose garden is weedy, sparse, and wilting.

- Failing students whose space is full of distractions.

Whatever it is that's going on in your life, there is always a clue to it within your space. It may be hard for you to see, because we're often blind to our own blocks and challenges. That's one of the reasons that I periodically consult someone else regarding my own Feng Shui! Even though I know a lot about Feng Shui, it's still often hard for me to notice my own patterns and clarify how to put them in check. A second set of eyes is always helpful.

I had one client who was a strong single woman who longed to be in a lasting relationship. Her bedroom was sparse and cluttered. She had a few small pictures on her wall of castles from locations where she had travelled. She liked the images because it reminded her of her travels which she enjoyed doing. They were certainly pretty but in no way represented the romantic love and partnership she was seeking. In fact, it took lots of talking and seeking but eventually it became clear that even though she sought partnership her heart was in fact very carefully protected. Kind of like it was locked away inside a castle fortress. It became clear that these images represented where she had gone because of past relationships but they were not representing where she was going. Even though she wished to change, these images were sending another message to herself and any prospective partners. We decided to move the images to her office as she aspired to organize travel groups one day. In the bedroom she looked for images that were more symbolic of love, togetherness and partnership. Along with clearing the space and spicing up the décor, changing out these are pieces was a subtle but powerful change for the space.

It's helpful to take a look at all the things you've chosen for your space from time to time. Notice if things still feel good. Pay attention to the subtle message various items give off to you. Be aware that we are always evolving and as our goals change so does our relationship with the things that surround us. Break up anything that is holding you in a pattern that you're ready to change!

Section One Credits

Five element chart, five element creative cycle, five element destructive cycle, five element controlling cycle, bagua map, individual guals, and floor plans were created and copyrighted by Marty McCagg.

HOME word wall hanging copyrighted by Coffee at pixabay.com.

SECTION TWO

Clearing Clutter and Removing Lower Energies

Section II – Introduction

In this section we'll discuss the concept of clutter within a space and how it affects the flow and Feng Shui for the occupants. We'll learn how to identify things in our space that don't serve us, release it with ease and then break up and disperse the remaining stuck energy and bless the space with intentions for the best outcomes.

8 The Clutter Effect

Clutter

The concept of clutter isn't really a Feng Shui concept. Accumulating possessions at a rapid fire pace is a recent predicament. In the developed world today, goods are easy to come by, disposable income is available, and we've fallen for the thought that having it all means being it all. It's simply easy to accumulate. But in Feng Shui terms, all of that accumulating stuff creates physical obstacles that alter the flow of chi.

Clutter affects the energy of a home and its occupants by slowing down and stagnating the Chi flow. It creates sluggish and confused energy which manifests as indecision and unnecessary commotion in the lives of the residents. Clutter can create a state of chaos that contributes to a lack of clarity and misperceptions. Taking care of so much stuff can be a factor in not having enough time elsewhere, and causing a sense of always falling behind. Holding on to items from the past can energetically keep you in the past, preventing you from being able to move forward. In reality, when clutter has accumulated in your space you literally become unable to create room for anything new to enter your life.

Where your clutter tends to collect is often a signal about what areas are troubling you. When vitality is not flowing in a particular life area it can often be reflected and noted by how you are keeping your environment.

Notice where your challenging spaces are. What area of the Bagua Map is affected? [See more about the Bagua Map in Chapter 5]. Is there one area in each room that presents a clutter challenge for you? Notice where it is in the Bagua of the room and you might gain some insight into what life area you are troubled by or avoiding.

Again, your home and your possessions are reflections of yourself. When clutter begins to accrue, it can be a signal of your own inner unrest and confusion over a subject. Physical clutter is often representative of emotional clutter. It's a clue that something is unsettled or there is some kind of chaos occurring within yourself. It can be a signal that you are confused, disconnected from spirit, suffering from fear, doubt or grief. Instead of dealing with these feelings, you fill your life with stuff to take care of. Then, in effect, you have to spend time worrying about, dealing with, and taking care of the stuff instead of facing your feelings.

As mentioned, my personal clutter tends to accumulate just inside the doorway of almost every room. Generally, this aligns with the career area of the Bagua Map in each room. It's a sure reflection of the challenges I face balancing a family and career, and maintaining boundaries between both. Over time, I've realized that most of the clutter is reflective of postponed decisions. It's all stuff I don't want to deal with right now so it just piles up and exponentially feeds the problem!

Remember that EVERYTHING has an energy force that radiates from it. Each item in your home has an individual vibration. You will be affected subliminally by, and will interact with, the energy of everything in your environment, either being drained by it or revitalized by it. With that thought in mind, it's not just about the amount of stuff, it's about the energy of it. If you are surrounded by things you love the energy is lighter and moves with more ease. In essence these uplifting items create good Chi in a space. If the stuff weights you down and feels complicated it's surely harder for the Chi to move around. It is depleting your Chi and causing other Chi to stagnate instead of being able to nourish the space and the occupants.

There is an incredible benefit to clearing out clutter. When you commit to eliminating items that are no longer serving you and only keep items that you love and that feed your soul, you are quickly rewarded with a flow of beneficial energy. You'll feel more energized and notice a greater sense of clarity. There will be an ease and grace about your life as vital Chi is able to reach and energize all of the life areas. You'll observe a greater sense of well-being once you begin to surround yourself with things you love and that support what you want in life. And most importantly, you'll create a space that allows you to anticipate and welcome new and exciting life opportunities. You'll create a space where you're better able to thrive!

What about other people's clutter?

Many times I get asked about what to do when others in the residence keep their space cluttered. First, you can't force clutter clearing on someone else. I'm sorry to say that I've made that mistake myself. When you force the issue, you can trigger lots of emotional distress for the affected parties. In addition to hard feelings, the reaction can cause them to hold on to stuff even tighter, and occasionally to replenish exponentially what has been discarded.

Instead, the best thing to do is to focus on eliminating your clutter and honoring your space and beloved items to the best of your ability. Keep your attention on the items that you can control and don't waste your energy on someone else's stuff or space. In a way, putting your attention on other people's stuff is a distraction that allows you to avoid making your own positive changes. By shifting and changing your part of the space you can be the example and hopefully encourage the others to change in their own time.

I've also been asked what you do when one family member wants to keep something that the other wants to let go. This is a tough call. My typical advice is that if one person really truly wants the item they should be allowed to keep it. Ideally, however, the item could be kept in a place that both can agree on. If a husband wants to keep that flashing neon beer sign, its best highlighted and honored in his workshop or man cave rather than right in the middle of the living room!

Stuff that might be considered clutter:

There are some items that my clients have had a challenging time letting go of. Here are some examples:

Books - Books hold lots of energy. They are like a good friend when no one else is around. Their constitution of paper makes them a wood element which is very absorbent of energy within a space. Books are very heavy and hard to move, without lots of physical effort and cost. It doesn't take long for a big library of books to "take root" on your bookshelves. People equate books with the stories, they fall in love with the characters like they are part of their lives, they remember the time-frame or memories associated with first reading the books, and they even get attached to the cover art as decoration. For some, books easily become prized possessions and part of collections. One of the problems is that the space to keep books is finite. After a lifetime of collecting them you eventually run out of room.

I remember one client who had two large walls full of books. She was an educator and scholar, so the books were like her stamp of approval. In her case we talked about how much energy they held and how releasing some would open up space for her to grow. This client valiantly went through her bookshelves and removed many, passing some on right away. Other books she chose to box up and find their right new owner. In the end it was too hard for her to let some of the books go. After weeks of driving around with the boxes in the car she conceded that she missed most of them and wanted to bring them back in. It was an A for effort in this case, because she did all the work and in the end realized which ones she truly loved and wanted to keep.

In my experience, people with lots of books tend not to move too often. I suspect in part it's because the thought and cost of packing and moving all those books is overwhelming!

Photographs - Ah! These are a challenge for me too. I've seen clients hunched over with a look of dread in their eyes at they look at boxes and boxes of photos from their life. They simply don't know where to begin. Going through photos takes a tremendous amount of time, as you look at each image and spend time with the memories. It's also a very emotional process of reliving past times with family and friends. The responsibility of organizing, labeling and handing down photos for historical purposes is usually a heavy task that puts people into overwhelm before they get started. It's a big but rewarding process.

Digital Information - Although digital information theoretically does not take up much physical space, it still has an energetic effect on our daily lives. This is another case where just because it's out of sight does not mean it's not out of mind or not having an impact. In fact, an overload of digital information can have a major impact on the clarity of your thoughts, your ability to accomplish a task, and the ease at which you can find what you need. Digital information includes inboxes loaded with unnecessary emails, hard drives full of out of date documents, and picture folders loaded with un-cataloged and duplicate images. All of this not-necessarily-useful digital media is multiplied by each added device! Tackling this kind of clutter is tedious, but moving forward with an organized system for the future is remarkably empowering.

Accessories – From shoes, belts, scarves and jewelry to accent our outfits to a linen closet stuffed with seasonally inspiring collections of accessories for the home, we're inundated with the things required to create the perfect look for our clothing and our décor. Usually each item matches something that is beloved, so it must stay in the collection. It may be hard to let go of that beautiful necklace that goes so perfectly with the dress you've worn once in the last 5 years, but, is it worth the time and energy its taking to hold onto it? Releasing the frills and embellishments can be hard because we're convinced they're necessary to make us feel put together. These are often the items that make us feel a little bit more lavish and extra special when we put them on. It can be hard to release these items because they usually total up to a substantial investment which is hard for some to let go of. Moving past these challenges is hard but goes a long way to simplifying a look, a décor, and daily life.

Gifts – So often, when I ask about the items on display in a home, I hear things like, "Oh, that was a present from my blah, blah, blah. It doesn't really match with the rest of my stuff but I just can't get rid of it because it was a gift." Oh. Yes. You. Can. Genuine gifts are not meant to be obligations. They are tokens of appreciation and recognition. Keeping an unloved item, even if it was a thoughtful gesture, does not do you or the gifter any good. In essence, it scrambles the energy between the two of you; it blocks the energy flow from moving. Instead, giving thanks for the item and releasing it to serve a better purpose is much more respectful of the giver than keeping something out of guilt. Letting the item go, to be loved and honored by someone else, frees up space for you and moves things forward for everyone: you, the giver, and the new receiver.

Memorabilia and collections – Having a collection of memorabilia or a specific item in your home is not necessarily having a home full of clutter. If you love your collection and having it brings you joy, then it certainly doesn't qualify as clutter. One thing I will stress is how you're honoring all of it. I've often been in homes that are so busy with a grouping of favorite things that none of it stands out. Sometimes too much is ... too much! The energy can't move around all of it. A crowded collection becomes hard to clean and is so congested that you can't really notice each piece anymore. To better honor a collection, break it up and switch things out seasonally. Each treasure will have more room, and can really be highlighted for a time rather than lost in the masses. Also, switching out the items occasionally will bring new Chi every time. It will be like opening presents on Christmas day every time you do it – fresh and exciting. Keep a collection if you like, but find a way to properly honor and show your love for each item without affecting your Chi flow.

I've walked into so many places to immediately notice a shelf full of some collectible: ceramic elephants, dolls, tea pots, shot glasses, etc. Of course the assumption is that the person loves the collection. Surprisingly, I often find out that they "used to love (insert collectibles)" but they don't so much anymore. Even so, friends and family keep gifting them new additions! They're ready to break the pattern and let this connection go but they feel obligated to display the new pieces – not because they love it but because they want to honor the gift. In the end I tell them that it's not honoring anyone to keep something that is no longer nourishing you. Let your friends know that you're over the fascination, and have passed the collectibles on to someone who loves and honors them more!

Belongings of a deceased loved one – Of course this is a tough one for people. Not only is it hard to let go of the stuff when it's all you have left to hold onto of the person you lost, but it's also tremendously emotional and overwhelming to simply start the process of letting go. These thoughts make it very difficult to consider letting things go. Some people hold onto items for years. Some never even move anything around. This is especially one of those times when waiting until you're ready is key. Baby steps are acceptable. Simply moving something slightly, or letting just a few innocuous pieces go, may allow trust that the ability to release the rest will happen in the right time. It's hard to believe that there will be life, love and happiness on the other side of holding on to those belongings. Ultimately the process is cathartic for most, but willfully leaping into those memories, emotions, fears, and realities takes remarkable courage.

With any of these types of potential clutter, letting go cold turkey can seem impossible. It's often helpful to simply box things up that you're unsure about for a month. Notice if you're missing any of it. At the end of the month, let anything go that you have not needed or missed during that time. Often people find that having the open space where stuff used to be, and extra time where they used to take care of that stuff, is much more appealing than what is in the box!

In a weird way, I believe that every item has a destiny, and it's possible you may just be the placeholder for that item until the receiver is ready to take it on. If you keep holding on to it, you are unhappy with it, while someone else may be unhappy not being able to find it. If it's not filling you up and energizing you anymore, let it go!

Not everything is clutter

If you've got a bunch of stuff that you simply aren't willing to let go of then it's not really clutter. Is it blocking your Chi flow? Probably. Is it keeping you from making room for something new? Possibly. But your inability to let it go easily is a sign that the stuff is still serving you by helping you feel safe, protected, worthy, etc. So cut yourself some slack and keep it. For now!

Trust that you'll be able to let go of the stuff when you're ready to. And it will be an easy process at the time. Allow yourself to become aware of the impact of the items. Notice the chaos and overwhelm. Finally, at some point, when the time is right, it will become more uncomfortable to manage the clutter than it will to begin the process of letting go. If you are badgered in to letting it go then the process will be tortuous and unhealthy. It's possible you'll react by accumulating as much more as quickly as you can after the unhealthy release.

It takes time

Clearing clutter is an ongoing process. We're constantly evolving and outgrowing things we thought we had to have. For best results, assess your possessions regularly. What you couldn't let go of last year will likely make the cut-list in future years. You'll know when it's time to evaluate when things start to feel cluttered to you, or when things simply feel stagnant in one or all of your life areas. You'll just know when it's time to start releasing.

I recently worked with someone who was ready to release things but was overwhelmed by the magnitude of the project. For years when her children were young they were her focus. After they were grown and off to college she realized there were many things she could release now that she had more time. It was not a fast process, but completed in stages over time. The beauty was that as she cleared the items away from her past she started to discover more clarity about herself, and what she truly wanted for the next phase of her life.

I can assure you that if you have clutter, hidden somewhere under all of it is a pile of what you really love and really want in life. You just can't see it right now! When you start to let go of the "used to need", "might need", "thought this would make me feel better" stuff you'll find clarity in what really makes you happy. When you release the items that are demanding energy from you but not reciprocating good feelings back you'll realize what's been draining you all along.

In releasing the extra stuff that is not nourishing you or bringing you satisfaction, you'll see how much better the extra time, extra space, and extra energy feel. But there's no doubt that tackling clutter that has built up for years will be an energetic and emotional commitment. There are lots of layers to work through when you start to release the ties you have to what you've kept and accumulated. In the next chapter we'll talk about why we find it hard to let stuff go, and discuss ways to release the emotion and energy associated with the stuff.

9 Releasing the Clutter to Uncover What You Really Love and Want

There's a big organizing kick these days. Every home magazine shows pretty pictures of closets full of stuff stored in pretty baskets and labelled. It sure looks better than a closet full of miscellaneous and mismatched bottles and boxes and linens. Is it more organized and easier to find what you need? Probably! Is the energy moving better around the stuff that's neat? Possibly! Is there less clutter impacting you and your space and your own energy? Probably not!

Organizing may make your stuff easier to find and may remove some chaos from your day as you're not losing and searching for things. But remember that all of that stuff has its own energy pattern and all of it still has an impact on you and your energy flow. Spending lots of money on tools, and lots of time putting stuff in its home is by no means as powerful of letting go of what is energetically weighing you down.

When you are in a space that is full of stuff (a little or a lot) that you *love* and that makes you happy and lifts you up your life will feel amazing! I've felt it myself and have seen it time and again with clients too.

For most of us (yes, me included) the process of assessing what to keep and letting go is a huge one. It takes lots of time, lots of commitment and lots of emotional energy to review our belongings and make a decision about what to keep. Not to mention figuring out where to put what you no longer want! Decluttering after a lifetime of accumulating is not an easy process but it is simultaneously empowering, healing and uplifting.

The good news is it doesn't all have to happen at once. In fact, it's probably better and easier to sustain if you approach it in small, inspired steps. In fact, the process of choosing to release anything from your life, anything at all, can open the flow and sway the energy enough for powerfully positive results. Start slowly. Start today! Seriously, pick a small project to work on soon. Choose one shelf on a book case you see often, or one drawer that you open daily, and quickly go through it, removing things that feel "eh." Things that are broken, that you don't love, or that feel heavy. Leave only things on that shelf that you *LOVE LOVE LOVE* looking at, and move the rest on. Now sit with it for a few days. Notice how good you feel about that one shelf. Notice how good you feel having made the change. Tomorrow pick a new shelf and do it again.

It's easy to fall into the comfort zone of reorganizing what you

> If I were to choose the three most important areas in the home to keep clutter free they would be:
>
> - The front door – where energy enters
>
> - The bedroom – where we spend the most time in a vulnerable state
>
> - The kitchen – center of health of the home
>
> In my experience, these are areas where clutter can have the most negative effect on the occupants of the space. So if you need to pick one spot to pare down, choose one of these areas first.

have or just moving things from one place to the other instead of actually taking action and creating change. One client I worked with was exhausted after spending tons of time and energy "clearing her clutter" over and over. It didn't take us long to figure out that she was just moving her stuff around and reallocating it rather than making a decision about it. Her clutter was a symptom of procrastination. The more time and energy she spent on the stuff, the less time she would have to work through the tough stuff that really mattered, like clarifying what she wanted in each area of her life!

On one occasion this client pulled a bunch of personal paperwork, journals and clippings that she had kept out from storage with the intention of paring it down. It had been stored for years and she had not referenced it or missed it. She moved it all to a spare room where she had more space to spread it out and go through it. But as she started looking through it all she became captivated by the nostalgia of it all. She released a few things but decided much of it was pertinent and she would reference it more often if it were easier to get at and more accessible so she purchased boxes to organize it in and filed it in a space downstairs. After expending all that time, energy and emotion on the papers that she had not needed for years, most of it was still there, still taking energy. Nothing had changed, it had simply moved.

No wonder this woman was exhausted and overwhelmed with her stuff/life. She was circling around and around and never really taking a new action. Either way she was expending energy but never fully releasing things. She just needed help getting out of this cycle and guidance and support in staying on track with the goal of letting go. In the end all it took was a push from someone that was impartial, and she easily released items and allowed the shift to take place.

Why it's hard to let it go:

When you begin the process of letting go of the things that no longer support you or that you don't love, it's important to recognize why you have trouble letting go of something. There are many typical clutter excuses that contribute to freezing up during the purging process.

I paid so much for it – It hurts to pay good money for something and then admit that it didn't work out for whatever reason. Maybe it didn't fit well after all, perhaps it didn't work as planned, and maybe, just maybe, it was a bad decision to buy it in the first place. Regardless, it is no longer working for you and it's depleting you, so it's best to accept this fact and let it go.

It's a waste to just throw it out – This is one of my own personal hot buttons! I have a hard time throwing away food, half used lotion, and even a tube of tooth paste with a couple of squeezes left in it. We are brought up being reminded not to waste; that we are lucky to have what we have; and easily reminded that there are others who aren't as lucky. These beliefs make us hold on to things that we don't need or aren't going to use and this creates clutter and stagnation in our life. Do your best to use things to their fullest. Pass unused stuff on to someone that can use it. But keep it moving. Someone out there could benefit from the stuff you're holding on to, but only if you release it.

It will just end up littering a landfill -- In this day and age it's hard to not be aware of the impact that human consumption has on the planet. I cringe every time my daughters come home from an afternoon at the local bowling alley/arcade with a bag full of little plastic toys that they won while playing. I know that they will forget about all of it in a few days and eventually will make it to the trash and a landfill.

Of course, the real solution is for all of us to become more mindful of the stuff we encourage and allow in our lives, but in the meantime, you can't sink under the weight of what you have already. Vow to be the change and no longer take on those trinkets. And in the meantime, do your best to ethically purge what you have. Recycle, reuse or pass it on where it might be more appreciated. Holding on to it to lessen your guilt over the environmental impact is creating an energy imbalance of another kind and does not serve your overall well-being. Release it and commit to not being part of the problem in the future.

I might need it later – I hear this one all the time. It's so easy to hold on to something that you think you might need at some point. Whether it's half a closet full of clothes you never wear but keep in case there's an occasion or the laundry room filled with a 10 year supply of fabric softener and dryer sheets, you still don't need to keep it! Aside from any financial cost, it's also costing lots of space, lots of time to care for, and drawing lots of energy from you. Let it go and trust that if the opportunity or need comes up you'll have what's necessary, or have the means to get it.

Letting go of what you "might" need means mustering up lots of trust in the synchronicity of things. It means believing that you'll always be in the right place at the right time with the right stuff. It's tough to release control and let the fates take their course. In fact, it usually takes some practice so give it a try by starting with something small. Release it and remind yourself that you trust that it will come to you when needed, or you'll be smart enough to seek out a substitute. It's hugely empowering to be able to do this – suddenly you don't have to hold onto things just in case and control every teensy factor involved! Talk about draining your energy. That's exhausting. Learn to release things and have faith in the divineness of this world. It's hard at first but incredibly freeing.

It was a gift – We touched on this in the last chapter. This is where we need to remember that it's the thought that counts, not the gift itself. When someone gives you a gift, it is the giving that makes them happy. Of course they've probably put time, money, and lots of thought into buying the perfect gift for you. That is the stuff that counts. The item itself really doesn't have any energy or relation to you until you add the friend and the gesture to it. Maybe the gift is perfect for you. Maybe you have the perfect spot for it. But if it isn't your favorite thing, or if you have nowhere to honor the item then it's not well served by keeping it. When someone gives a gift it's because giving feels good. It brings them joy to give it. It pretty much ends there. They certainly would not feel good knowing that the item they gave you is not bringing you joy or is holding you back in some way. There is no friend contract that says you must love all gifts received and keep all gifts while displaying them in a place of honor forever and ever! And a good friend would not want you holding on to something they gave you simply to make them feel better. Personally I forget what I've given very quickly.

Where are you now?

It's also helpful to recognize where you are in the process of holding on to things. Are you already eagerly moving it on? Having a hard time deciding what you should keep and what you should let go of? Or are you simply too overwhelmed to start the process at all? Remember that in some ways maintaining the clutter or the constant and time consuming struggle with clutter is somehow serving you. Consider what the struggle is helping you avoid or what its keeping you from. Perhaps you're not ready to move forward but awareness will get you on the path.

It's easy to forget that our stuff is just stuff. It's not memories or emotions. It only takes on these feelings when you make it possessions. I recently listened to someone talk about clearing out some furniture from her grandparent's house after they had passed. There was a hutch that she remembered fondly. She remembered the hutch at family gatherings for years. The hutch was always present, holding her grandmother's prized possessions and watching over all the happenings. In fact, the woman recalled that the hutch appears in almost all of the family photos taken in the house. She was very attached to the piece because of these connections. While other family members considered this piece clutter – it was no longer serving them – it was certainly not clutter to her. She had attached positive memories and emotions to the piece. To her family it was junk but to her it was treasure. Either way, it's still just a hutch!

Noticing what emotions are being reflected in the clutter or feeling the emotions fully when you start to deal with the clutter is pivotal in the process. Often people will recognize scarcity, doubts, fears, avoidance, overwhelm, chaos, blame, loss, guilt, and indecision come up when they begin the process of letting go. It can be so disconcerting that they freeze, and tuck the stuff and the emotions back away again. Instead, if you sit with the emotions and seriously consider them and the impact of the stuff, it will dissipate and lose its power over you. And then it's easy to release, and easy to let go. The lightness and relief after this process can't be understated! Energy levels, attitudes and outcomes in various life areas are positively shifted.

Tricks to make letting go easier

As you read this book you may be becoming more aware of what you're surrounded by and whether or not it's serving you. You may be feeling uncomfortable with what you see and overwhelmed by what you feel and how to make it better. Even though the process can seem daunting, it's well worth taking it on. The process of letting go can be positive, facing the memories and emotions is empowering, and the results can be life changing! Here are some ways to help you move through the road blocks and start moving on the things that no longer serve you:

Consider the end result

When you're feeling stuck about letting things go, or deciding what things to let go of, consider the end result. Consider whether you're going to need that thing again. What's the worst thing that will happen if you let it go and then do need it after it's gone? How easily can you replace it later? Could you borrow one for the time you need it, can you find the information elsewhere?

Also take a moment to think about your space after you've cleared unsupportive items. Consider how that cleared out space will feel. Notice how you will be able to honor the items that you have decided you do love and have chosen to keep. Imagine walking into your newly opened space and seeing only things that you love. It's gonna be great!

Imagine the best result for the item

Which clutter to keep exercise

Close your eyes, take a few slow deep breaths. In your mind's eye, choose a possession and look at it. Imagine picking it up and holding it. Notice how it looks and how it feels as you consider all things about it. Is it in good shape or disrepair? Can you recall when you last used it, admired it or even noticed it? Consider what purpose it is serving you now. What memories does it bring about for you? What emotions come up as you look at it? (Ideally you feel love, fulfillment and joy from it!) Take a moment to check in with your body and breathe as you keep considering the item. Are you feeling lifted up by it, or weighed down by it? Now take it a bit further and start a conversation with your chosen piece. Ask it why it's come to you. Ask whether you should keep it. And if you should keep it ask it where and how it wants to be kept and honored. If it's clear to let it go, then consider asking where it should go. This is a great exercise that lets you take your own thoughts out of the process and instead tap into your innate intuition and divine guidance system. It's pretty powerful in helping you get started.

When you're struggling with letting an item go, take some time to imagine who will receive what you're giving up. Visualize someone else enjoying it and putting it to good use. If it makes you feel better, pass it on to someone where you can still see the good it's doing. I had a hard time giving up my daughters' baby clothes and toys but I gave them to a younger family member that was starting her own family. It was fun to get to see her daughter wearing their dresses and giving their toys new life.

Just start somewhere

Most importantly, just start the motion. Giving things away opens up room and allows space to receive. Even just clearing out a drawer can shift and start moving the energy in mysterious and supportive ways. You won't be able to predict what opportunities this will create but I assure you that you'll notice positive change and rewards from the practice of decluttering.

10 Energetically Clearing a Space with Smudging

Clearing unseen energies

Smudging is a powerful technique that has been used for centuries in many cultures to clear out negative energies in a space. You may have removed items that had negative associations attached, but there is often a residual negative energy still left in a space. These unseen and subliminal forces that linger in a space leave an imprint and have an effect on occupants if not addressed. The process of clearing this unseen lower energy from a space is called Space Clearing or Energy Clearing.

There are Feng Shui Professionals that specialize in this one technique, and entire books are written on this process itself. Through the years I've studied and practiced several techniques and have come to streamline my own process which is presented here. This process is best undertaken after you've had a chance to release clutter and anything that no longer serves and before you add enhancements to a place. It's especially good to do a clearing after any negative event in the space, whether it be an argument, challenging visitors, a stressful project, or especially following an illness or death to help clear the residual energies that accompany such strife.

Preparations for smudging

The process of clearing and blessing a space can be as ceremonious and sacred as you choose to make it. I will say from experience that the more care you put into preparing for it, the more successful it will be. Many suggest taking special care to clean and protect yourself and anyone else present before starting the energetic clearing. Gather the tools needed including a drum or bell, a stick of dried sage, matches, a bowl of water, and chosen essential oils, or fresh fruits, flowers or herbs. Some people are very particular about the tools they use for this process. Choose something that resonates well and feels right to you. You might choose to set up an altar to stage your tools and to work from, adding flowers, candles, and crystals to a space in the center of the house. You can ask for guidance and support during the clearing from any deities or guides that you call on. In my experience, this is a powerful and transformative energetic process which you can choose to individualize as you see best.

Breaking up heavy and stuck chi

Begin by opening the doors and windows. Good ventilation of the space is necessary to start circulating air and Chi through all the spaces to be worked on and to allow an exit for unwanted essences. Dust and dirt are magnets for lower energies to cling to, so sweeping these away will begin the process of shaking up these heavier vibes. Give the entire space a thorough cleaning, including shaking out rugs and drapes if possible.

Next, move through the space slowly, making loud noises to further break up the hidden and stuck forces. Clap your hands, ring a bell, bang on a drum or a gong, play a singing bowl or use any other tool that will pleasingly and sufficiently shake things up. The goal is to send vibrations into the space and get things moving where they have been heavy or stuck. Pay extra attention to corners, crevices, low and high places. If you notice your instrument falling flat it can often be a sign of stagnant energy, stay there until it feels in tune again and then move on. When the energy has been broken up sufficiently the sound will resonate freely and the area will feel lighter.

Go through the rooms a second time, this time carrying a bundle of sage that has been lit enough so that there is smoke rising from it. Allow the scent of the sage and the smoke to permeate all areas of the space. In ancient traditions it is believed that the smoke lifts and carries away the lower energies from the space, cleansing, clearing, and purifying it as it goes. If you don't have a bundle of sage available, you can substitute with burning incense, diffused essential oils, or simply move on to the next step.

Bestow positive blessings

Finally, repeat your steps again this time carrying a bowl of water that has been infused with pure therapeutic grade essential oils, fresh herbs, fresh flowers, or even the fresh peels of citrus fruits. As you move through the house dip your fingers, (or a feather if you prefer), into the water and sprinkle it around, thanking and blessing each area as you go.

I promise your home will feel SO GOOD after taking the time to do this ritual of Space Clearing. I do this 3-4 times a year, usually around the New Year, after a good spring cleaning, and in the early fall.

Using salt to absorb energies

Another trick to clearing lower energies is to place bowls of high quality salt crystals in any area that has stagnant or stressed energies. Leave the salt there overnight and then dispose of it outside the house, properly returning it to the earth. Use caution when discarding the salt, choosing a location it away from the home, play areas, pet areas, and gardens.

After taking time to perform a space clearing on your rooms, you have a completely clean slate to work with energetically. Now you can really use what you've learned about Feng Shui to enhance your space and direct the positive energies into the area of your life that need it most.

SECTION THREE

Hidden Meaning in our Homes

Section III – Introduction

Aside from the architectural functions of each part of a house – doorways to lead in and out, closets to store items, hallways as passageways – different areas of the house also have deeper symbolic meanings in Feng Shui.

In this section we'll cover how aspects of your home can be correlated to your physical body or your spiritual and soul state. You'll learn that the way you keep these spaces can be directly related to the way you keep yourself.

Finally, we'll review the ideal arrangement for each of these spaces according to Feng Shui and any special considerations for each room. Ideally, once you learn these hidden meanings of your home and how it relates to you, your body and/or your life, you become much more conscious of how you're taking care of each area of your home, and able to honor every space as needed.

Remember that everything in your home will either increase your energy and vitality or diminish i.!

11 Front Door and Entry Area

~ Transition Between Public and Private Sides ~

~Mouth of Chi ~ Energy Source for Entire Home ~

In addition to being a physical transition space between outside and inside, this space also represents the transitional space between your outside self (the public side of yourself that you share with others) and your inside self (your private life). This is the place that sets the energy for your entire home/life.

In Feng Shui, the front door is called the "mouth of Chi." It's where all vital life energy enters into your home. Symbolicall it is also where all opportunity (aka chi) "come knocking."

Front doorway

If you're home isn't easy to find, or is unapproachable or unwelcoming, then fresh, vital Chi and even potential opportunity could pass you by. The reasons to make your front entrance Feng Shui friendly are really just common sense. If the delivery driver can't find your address, you may not receive an expected package. If a long lost friend decides to drop by for a visit but gets uneasy as they approach your entrance, you may miss an opportunity for connection. And of course, in a situation where you need help, emergency services need to be able to find you quickly, before tragedy strikes. Your home should be accessible so that any potential prospect can safely and easily find you.

© Sarah Commerford

When considering your house in terms of Feng Shui, it can be helpful to pretend that you are approaching your house for the first time as a guest/stranger. Make your home easy to find with clearly marked numbers. Help lead the way to your door by creating an open path to the front door, painting the door an attractive color, and highlighting the entrance with flower pots or other markers. Add lighting as needed so the approach to the house is clear and safe at night.

Create a feeling of warmth and hospitality by adding welcoming elements like a welcome mat and wreath on the door.

Consider all of these elements together and note whether you feel good as you get ready to enter the front door. Remove or hide anything that is distracting or interfering with the welcoming space you're trying to create. Make sure the door is easy to open and not blocked or hindered from opening all the way.

Door #1 or Door #2?

Frequently there is confusion when there are two entrances to the house. The "architectural" front door is the showpiece that is meant to formally welcome guests inside. However, often there is also a secondary door that is more functional and often more convenient to use. Someone approaching for the first time has to hesitate and decide which door is the right one to approach. The energy that this situation consistently creates in the house is uneasiness and indecisiveness.

In a perfect world, if all homes were designed with Feng Shui in mind, these energetic frustrations could be avoided. In the meantime, the way to correct it is to do the best you can to make it clear which doorway people (and chi) should approach. It's always best to direct people to the architectural front door when possible. This can be done by making the real front door stand out. Use lighting, welcome signs, and even attractive baskets of flowers to highlight the main entry. You may even want to downplay the second doorway or even somehow hinder access to it. Signage works great in this instance. A small "please use front door" sign hung on the secondary door will immediately alleviate confusion.

I remember working with one client who lived in a split entry house. Basically they had two front doors just feet apart from each other. The secondary door was the most convenient door, located at the driveway level. The main door was accessed by going up a set of stairs from the driveway. The owner told me, "No one ever knows which door to go to when they come here! And when the doorbell rings I end up running to the front door, then down to the lower door, and most of the time back up to the front door again to catch the person before they leave." Who wants to deal with that kind of frustration every time the doorbell rings! To ease this irritation, we simply highlighted the main door and downplayed the secondary door. Family members could still use the second door, but it was much clearer to newcomers which door should be used, because it's best to direct company and deliveries to the front door whenever possible.

When you have a secondary door that you prefer to use for convenience sake, you can certainly keep using it, but find a way to use the front door often too. For example, it's common for families to pull the car into the garage and then enter the house via the garage. Often there is no reason to use the front door at all. If this is the case, make it a daily habit to open the front door and move in and out of it for any small errand including watering the plants or checking the mail. This will do a lot to bring flow and fresh Chi into your space.

Inside entryway

What's inside the front doorway has an impact as well. It's helpful to have a place to stop upon entering, to adjust to the new surroundings, to put down your stuff and "shed the energy from the outside world" before going further.

Step inside your front door and take some time to consider how comfortable you feel. Do you look around and look forward to going further, or do you feel uneasy instead?

© Sarah Commerford

Ideally, the space is well lit, organized and appealing. Notice if there are any sights, sounds or smells that are off-putting, and remedy them. A coat tree, basket for shoes, and hooks for keys and personal items are all considerations here. Finally, consider how clear it is which way to go once you're inside. Lighting, carpets, and decorative focal points can all be used to ease the way in.

Summary

In Feng Shui terms, I would say that the front entryway is the most important area to address. This is where I focus whenever I need some fresh energy in any area of my life. Whether it's more cash flow, new clients, or insight on a problem, reviving the entrance area always sets things in motion!

12 Windows

~ Eyes of the Home ~ Clarity ~

~ Ability to See Things Clearly in Life ~

~ Symbolize Perception and Thinking ~

In Feng Shui terms, windows are much more than architectural features of the house. They are considered the "eyes" of the home and your personal windows to the world. They are symbolic of clarity and your ability to see things clearly in life. Often they can be a mirror into your own perception and thinking (clear or not!).

When windows are clouded or dirty it can often reflect clouded thinking or an inability to make decisions. Dirty clouded windows can often manifest as having a distorted view of whatever is going on around you. In a way it can be like looking through life with tinted glasses – our perception becomes just a little bit colored.

Ideally windows are safe, in good working order, clean, and have coverings that help regulate chi, light and air flow.

© Kerri Miller

Windows are our eyes to the outside world. By day, uncovered windows let us to see what's going on outside, but others can't easily see in. By night, uncovered windows allow others to see in, but we can't see out. In this way windows have a powerful impact on our privacy and sense of security. Windows are also openings where vital Chi can easily flow in and out, impacting the space and occupants. Furnishings near windows, things hung in the window and window coverings can all be used to balance and regulate the Chi flow to keep it in the home to nourish the occupants longer.

How a space feels is greatly influenced by the number and placement of windows. If there are too many windows in a space, you may feel anxious and exhausted: vital Chi is escaping out through them. If there are not enough windows in the space, the occupants can feel depressed and weary; there is not enough fresh Chi circulation.

Have you ever walked into a room where the drapes have been drawn and doors closed off for a period of time? This may often be done to prevent fabrics and woodwork from fading from the sunlight or to help regulate extremes in temperature. As soon as you walk into these rooms, you can feel the coldness, heaviness, and stagnancy. The space is depressed because no fresh energy is flowing. Opening up the blinds and the windows, if possible, for at least a few hours a day makes a big difference in raising the Chi in a space. Sunlight and fresh air are powerful Chi enhancers – they are chi! This vital energy flows into the space and is very helpful in "casting light" and giving you a fresh perspective.

Although keeping windows clean is no easy feat, having a clear view is significant. Even if the windows don't seem dirty, often one of the most powerful things you can do when you are seeking clarity on a subject is to wash the windows inside and out! I've done this myself many times when looking for direction on a topic and I am always amazed how clear things can become in my mind as I clean.

Ideally you want to look out onto a pleasant setting from each window. Create a positive focal point outside, by adding seating areas, fountains, outdoor structures, garden beds, potted plants, bird feeders, or lights to uplift the view from the windows. I once toured a home where the homeowner had done a tremendous job beautifying the view from each window. Even outlooks that had once been a blank nook facing another wall of the house were turned into little seating areas with bird feeders and benches. These views made the entire inside of the house even more pleasing.

Safety is always a consideration with windows; they should open and close easily and be safe to be around. I've been in the upper floors of some homes, standing in front of floor to ceiling windows, and it felt very uneasy. In one particular case there was a large, very high window in an adolescent's room located on the third floor of a house. This child suffered from debilitating anxiety. When standing in front of this window I felt like I could fall right out; the angle of the view and the overall height was unsettling. I felt it was contributing to the child's troubles, so I encouraged the parents to install a safety gate and partially cover/block the lower half of the window to make the child feel safer. Paying attention to and trusting those subliminal signals your body gives you can often solve many issues related to Feng Shui.

In another situation, a client had windows with broken springs, so the windows were nearly impossible to open, and then, once open, would slam shut unless propped up. Imagine that daily – fighting to open it, jumping back to safety as it slammed shut – and consider how that affected the energy of the house and the client's personal energy day after day. If they are in good working order, windows can powerfully enhance Chi flow, but if they are not safe or working properly they can have a detrimental energetic effect.

Regulating the Chi flow through windows

Be aware of how the windows in the space affect the flow of Chi through your house. Chi naturally wants to exit through the easiest route, so you may decide to keep some windows closed to prevent Chi from escaping too quickly. It's important to maintain windows so that vibrant Chi can't seep out through them. Repairing broken glass and screens, as well as caulking to shore up the efficiency of the windows is important in a good Feng Shui'd home.

Window coverings are helpful in balancing the number of windows, regulating the amount of light and Chi that flow through them, and allowing for privacy when needed. Window treatments can let light in during the day but also allow for privacy inside the space at night. They can also work to complement the décor and elemental balance of the room. If you have an unpleasant view (like another building or a barren street) and can't make changes to this outside space, then blinds, drapes, or other window treatments can be placed to keep your attention inside.

If you have a window directly opposite your front door, the Chi coming in the door might sneak right out again, through the window across from it. The best solution is to deflect and slow down the chi. This can be done by laying ornate carpeting on the floor, placing furniture or a plant in line, keeping window décor partially closed, or hanging faceted glass crystals or other window ornaments/sun catchers on or in front of the window.

Finally, consider what furniture you place in front of a window. Furnishing are good to slow down Chi from escaping, but if a person is seated in a chair in front of a window or sleeping on a bed in front of a window then they are at risk of their own personal Chi being carried out the window. Be wary of this when placing furniture around windows.

Summary

In Feng Shui terms, windows are much more than architectural features of a room. They're symbolic of the thoughts we have and the clarity and vision with which we see the world. Take a look at your windows with fresh eyes and make any needed adjustments to keep your view uplifting and the Chi flowing in a nourishing way around your rooms.

13 Living Room

~ Gathering Space ~ Connection to Family ~

~ Connection to Community ~

Living rooms, family rooms and play rooms are similar in that they are active rooms.

Generally, they are more yang than other spaces of the house because activity is happening and lots of people are in the space.

Ideally these spaces are attractive, comfortable, inviting, and facilitate communication between occupants of the space.

Living rooms

Historically, the living room was where the family came together after a busy day and a hearty meal. Families would gather in front of the hearth and spend time together. The fireplace was the customary focal point in historic homes. Members would gather around it to keep warm and share their day's experience while reading, knitting, playing a game or relaxing. Back in the day, there weren't many other places to go after dinner, unless you went to bed, so everyone came to the parlor to be together.

© Kerri Miller

Living rooms are meant to be social and active spaces where people can come together and BE together. The placement of the furniture should encourage connection between people in the space, with seats positioned so everyone can comfortably see and hear each other. I've been into many living spaces where all of the furniture is placed against a wall with lots of open space in between the furnishings. It may look pretty but it's not doing much to facilitate bonding between those gathered in the room. No wonder family members are distant and aloof to each other, it takes too much energy to connect from such a distance.

The living room is where guests would traditionally be led into when visiting, so it's also a place to express yourself and show off your personality. Place things in this space that you are willing to share about yourself with guests and company. Colors, family photos, and artwork can all show off a little about who you are and what your family members find important. Consider how the objects and décor in your living room support the side of you that you want people to see.

Use it or lose it

In larger homes today, formal living rooms often become extra, unused spaces. Even during gatherings, these spaces can be passed by as people gather in more comfortable and casual spaces like the kitchen, dining area or family room. If your living room is empty and lonely, consider what else you could use it for. I've seen living rooms converted into game rooms, libraries, home offices, and music rooms. It's important to use all areas of a home, so that Chi flows into all the life areas. Consider how you can use the space so that it's an active and essential part of your home.

Family rooms

© Sarah Commerford

Sometimes in homes today, there is a "formal living room", only used when company comes, and the family gathers in a less formal "family room." This is a versatile and fun room where everyone can come together and play or relax. The function and energy of this room tends to be much more casual and relaxed than the formal living room. It's generally a place where active energy possessions like toys and electronics are welcome! The purpose of this room is still connection, and hopefully it's a space where the family can be together while also pursuing individual activities (one person may be knitting, another watching TV, another doing homework, while others play a game).

Family rooms work best if they are durable, safe, comfortable, and can accommodate everyone's needs. Lots of color and art are encouraged here! Think about all the things your family does when they come together and try to make space for it be used, and storage for it when it's not in use. Create easy storage for toys or games so the space can be "picked up" quickly in between uses. Consider storing electronics, including TV's, computers and other devices inside a cabinet when not in use. This not only helps minimize energetic interference from their electronic source, but also lessens some of the addictive power they can have over us.

Whether your space is formal or casual, consider where attention is directed in the room. Ideally, the space still encourages that sense of togetherness. This can prove more of a challenge with today's technology replacing the quiet, warm fireplace that was the traditional focus. Today's modern day focal points like televisions, laptops, iPads and smart phones actually have the ability to transport our attention to other places and people entirely. Even when gathered in the same room, each person can be focused on something different. This divided attention span stretches and strains the connection of the family unit. A mindfully arranged room can help alleviate some of these present day challenges by limiting or directing the focus to a degree.

Pull up a chair

Take time to sit in each seat in the room. How does it feel? What do you see while you are seated there? Is it easy to communicate with others seated around you? Is it easy to get to the seat to sit down or is it blocked or challenging? Ideally each seat is inviting and accessible and your largest piece of furniture will have a commanding view of the entrance to the room. If anything feels off, try shifting, moving things, or taking things away until it feels more comfortable. Also, consider the view that commands the most attention. Often it's the TV, which makes occupants focus on the screen rather than each other. You get to decide the kind of interactions you want in the space and can set it up to encourage the activities that you prefer.

Summary

Although it's a challenge to maintain connections in today's world, Feng Shui can be used to encourage interaction and define focal points in living rooms and family rooms.

14 Kitchen and Dining Room

~ Heart of the Home ~ Kitchens ~

~ Symbol of Wealth, Abundance, and Health ~ Gathering Space ~

In Feng Shui, kitchens are considered strong symbols of wealth. A kitchen stocked with abundant foods can nourish and sustain the whole family.

Kitchens also symbolize health, as the kind of food prepared in the kitchen has a great impact on the health and well-being of the family.

Ideally kitchens are clean, clutter free, well-stocked, in good working order, and provide support and good work flow for the chef.

Have you ever hosted or attended a house party and noticed that all of the guests are crammed into the kitchen? Kitchens naturally have an active and magnetic energy that draws people in. Everyone wants to be there (and often everything gets dumped there!) People gather there to eat, socialize, and even do homework! Kitchens are where we come together to start the day and where we meet again after a long day. The kitchen truly is the energetic heart of the home so keeping a good vibe in the space is important.

© Sarah Commerford

A kitchen with good Chi flow will be supportive of the chef, making the tasks flow smoother. An energized and happy chef will have plenty of love (aka good chi) to put into the food. I do believe that the more lovingly food is prepared the more nourishing it is to eat! This affects the vitality of the food served positively, further nourishing the occupants in the home. Having a good Feng Shui'd kitchen goes a long way to supporting health, but it also improves the start and finish to each day. This makes it even more important to take a conscious look at the space. Simple changes can often make the space feel better and flow better so that hard tasks can be lightened and more pleasant.

Obviously, for many, a complete Feng Shui friendly kitchen renovation is out of the question. But there are some things you can do to make your kitchen more attractive, functional, and pleasant. Enhancing a few key areas will make a big difference in the functionality and feel of the whole space, improving Chi flow and better nourishing everyone that frequents the space.

Refrigerator, pantry, and cupboards

The refrigerator and pantry are where we keep all of the food that will sustain us until it is ready to be prepared. These places are like bank vaults for very precious items. Think of how much of our income we spend on food and how much it contributes to sustaining a healthy life. Our food truly is valuable, and the place where we keep it is important. This is not a space where we want stale and stuck energy, because that will reflect on the meals prepared and ultimately in our own health and well-being.

Keeping these spaces clean and organized is vital to keeping the energy of the space fresh. Items stored here should be easy to find when needed. This will smooth the task of preparing a meal and ensure the staples turn over often enough so they are consumed at their freshest, most vital (most Chi filled!) point. No one wants to throw food away after spending good money on it, so keeping things cycling through the kitchen storage areas is crucial.

If better health and wellness is a goal for you then the kitchen refrigerator and pantry are the first places to look. Stock them with foods that support the level of health and wellness you're trying to achieve. If you want to make a healthy change in your diet it will be very challenging if you don't first purge items from your kitchen that don't support that new goal. Inspire yourself to maintain health goals every time you enter the kitchen by bringing in only items that feel good.

Cluttered cupboards create a mood that is frustrated and disorganized and result in a less efficient space. Even if the doors are closed, if it's cluttered and messy inside its still having an effect on you and the space. We live in a culture that encourages "stocking up" but often we don't use all that we buy right away and it sits there collecting dust and blocking the energy from flowing. Ideally we're using whatever we bring in quickly and replacing it. This is the goal of flow. Add in too much "just in case stuff" and things can't move effectively.

This is true for kitchen tools too. Make sure to eliminate any pots, dishes, appliances and kitchen tools that are not in good working order or are not needed often. Keep only what is needed, loved, and makes work in the kitchen easier. Some items in your cabinets like platters and roasting pans that are only used for holidays, and bulk staples, might better be stored in a closet or the basement until needed. Some of my less frequently used serving ware and appliances are stored in the laundry room!

Because the kitchens and dining spaces are such "hotspots" they also tend to collect everything! ... mail, receipts, toys, homework,

The 80/20 rule

Use the 80/20 rule in cabinets ... 80% full, 20% empty space. Otherwise when you come home with new groceries they'll have nowhere to go and the clutter problem will begin again. This also allows you to see and find what you need easily, and prevents buying duplicates of items you already had but couldn't find.

keys, gadgets, etc. It's important to arrange your kitchen so that this stuff can easily be moved to a permanent home, giving you a clean slate for creatively prepping good food and good times. Notice what is consistently collecting in your kitchen and dining spaces. See if you can find a more permanent space for that stuff to land. If you don't use something every day, then put it away. Since I no longer drink coffee every day, my coffee maker is stored away until company visits.

Stove

The stove is one of the most important areas in Feng Shui because it represents the fire element and is further symbolic of health and wealth. The area where the stove is placed should be an energetically sound space – this is where you are preparing all of the food to nourish and energize your family so you want the energy to be good. Ideally the stove is positioned to allow the chef a view of the kitchen and entryway, and to encourage interaction with family and guests while cooking. In the West, most stoves are positioned to face a wall, so placing a mirror on the backsplash above the stove is encouraged. This makes the stove more comfortable to work at and also symbolically "doubles" the burners, which are symbols of wealth. Magnifying the positive energy of the stove is a powerful traditional Feng Shui enhancement that can have substantial benefits.

Keeping the stove clean and in working order is of critical importance. It's tempting to see this element as a workhorse in the kitchen, and a replaceable or repairable appliance, but energetically it's a symbol of wealth and health. Not taking care of the stove is reflective of not taking care of those aspects of your life. The simple act of making sure it is clean is symbolic. Safety is clearly a big issue too, which is why it's important to keep the stove in safe working order. Make it a strong symbol of health and wealth by keeping the stove clean and its energy auspicious.

Dining area or eating space

Dining rooms and other eating spaces symbolize the abundance and joy of coming together for a sustaining meal. Ideally these spaces are welcoming, uplifting and celebrated places.

The eating space in the kitchen is truly important. Perhaps you have a separate dining room where meals are enjoyed, so some of this will apply there too. In addition to meals, the kitchen table can also be a hotbed of other activity including crafting, playing a game, putting together a puzzle, working or studying. Ideally, this space is conducive to slowing down and coming together. Creating a space that is comfortable, serene and focused to allow distraction free meals or activities will positively affect the togetherness and communication of the family unit.

In today's fast paced world, it's easy for the eating table to become a clutter zone or a dust collector instead. This is symbolic of not slowing down long enough to rest, refuel and connect. Especially when daily life feels too hectic, consider committing to using this space regularly, even if it's only once a week, for a meal or activity where everyone

is present and participating. This space gives us the opportunity to slow down, focus on ourselves and each other, and create a sacred time and space to come together for a meal and to share experiences.

© Sarah Commerford

I have one client who shared how her in-laws set the table elegantly with nice table linens, china, glassware, candles, and centerpieces for every single meal. What a symbolic, Chi enhancing act! It's a way of making every single bite of food and moment together more sacred. It's clearly a huge energetic shift when you take this time to make a space and a setting extra special. For a busy family this might be too much to take on, but there's always the option to have one extra special meal or activity a week where everyone comes together.

To encourage people wanting to gather easily in the space, consider what kind of furniture is in place here. The shape of the table affects how people come together. A rectangle table or oval table will create a much different interaction than a breakfast bar where everyone faces in the same direction. Finally, consider the art and enhancements around this space. Since this is a space to nourish the body and soul, consider feeding all the senses at each meal or gathering with music, flowers, candles, and comfortable seating.

Consider every angle

Sit in each chair and consider how comfortable it is, and if your view is pleasant from each spot. Make sure each seat is easy to get in and out of without bumping into things (round or oval tables are preferred for this reason). Also consider where people are seated. Who is in the most commanding position of the table/room with a sturdy wall behind them and a view of the table/room? The person seated here will be in the most supported place and will have more weight in the relationships. If family dynamics are challenging, moving seats around can be a great way to regain balance and equality amongst family members.

Summary

So now it's clear why kitchens are so important in Feng Shui terms. Use your new Feng Shui knowledge to enhance this space to support your family's health and wealth. Make your kitchen the heart of the home, where you connect with all that sustains you and create strong interactions.

15 Bedroooms

~ Inner Self ~ Private Life ~

~ Gateway to Sleep ~ Space for Healing ~

~ Rejuvenation ~ Physical Love ~

Bedrooms are symbolic of our inner self, our personal essence once all the labels and identities and roles (like wife, brother, son, etc.) are removed.

Bedrooms are a gateway to sleep, a space of healing, and a place for romantic connection and physical love.

They are our private space, where we can be most true to ourselves, our life purpose, and our clearest values.

Bedrooms are a place to honor the union we have in relationships.

Ideally, bedrooms are comfortable, soothing, restful, and foster connection with your inner self, and your partner.

Creating space for rest and rejuvenation is of critical importance if we are to thrive in all areas of our life. How can we thrive if we are yawning and dozing off because we haven't slept well? How can we move forward in all areas of life if we are stuck struggling with insecure relationships? Making adjustments to your bedroom space so that it supports restoration and connection is one of the most beneficial Feng Shui changes you can make. The time spent creating sacred and deliberate space in this room will have a strong positive impact on all areas of your life.

Rest and rejuvenation

We spend nearly 1/3 of our life sleeping in our bedrooms. During this time, we are in our MOST vulnerable energetic state! The energy and Chi surrounding us while we are sleeping has a huge impact on our quality of life, productivity, relationship, and overall health.

© Kerri Miller

These days, more than half of all adults suffer from some type of sleep difficulty at least a few nights a week. Watch all the ads on TV or take a walk down the sleep support aisle at the pharmacy, and you'll see plenty of products being marketed that encourage sleep at night or ease sleepiness in the day. Room aesthetics can play a big role in supporting sleep. Room layout, temperature, lighting, sound, furnishings, and linens can all be used to create a space that is comfortable and conducive to sleeping well.

Consider ways that you can make this space calm and cozy, warm and romantic. Plush fabrics, supportive mattresses, ambient lighting, and soothing music are all ways to create a restful sanctuary. There are already plenty of active spaces in our homes where TVs, laptops, paperwork, laundry, and treadmills are welcome, so hopefully they are not in the bedroom. If they must be there, take measures to conceal these items while you sleep so they will not be so actively distracting you while you recharge and reconnect.

Romance and passion

On top of lost sleep, there is also a widening gap in our romantic relationships. Couples are separating or seeking therapy in growing numbers. Experts warn that lack of communication, lack of intimacy, and simple lack of spending time together are all big threats to relationships.

Our lives are busy and generally too full of activity and technology. We simply don't give ourselves time or space away from the busy-ness. This 24/7 action has started to creep into our bedroom and inch out the quality of time and space that we give to rest ourselves and nurture our personal relationships. Just as in the kitchen where we have to create the time and setting for family connection, we can also use the bedroom to create the time and the space to focus on our partnerships.

In one home, I could guess right away that the client's marriage was taking a hit after having kids. I knew this by simply reading the signs in their space and noticing where all the attention was going. It was clear there was plenty of love, organization, and endearment in the children's spaces. Yet the spaces shared by the parents were stark and disorganized in comparison. There was no artwork, the shades were drawn, the laundry not put away, and the furniture looked like hand-me-downs from a college apartment. It was clear that no energy was being spent on this room, and the marriage was reflecting this. This couple needed to invest in themselves in order to support the central part of the family unit.

A bedroom can be deliberately designed to emphasize the priority of the relationship. It's the perfect place to escape from the hectic pace of the outside world and create time to quietly reconnect. There are plenty of active zones in our home to do our busy-ness! Be vigilant and allow in only items that encourage connection, including comfortable areas to be together and images and symbols that support unity and romance.

Remember that this is your private space. No one else needs to see what's in here so you can really showcase your romantic and passionate side in the décor. If your relationship is feeling stale and strained, take a look at the bedroom. Consider how warmer tones, silkier fabrics and sensual artwork could inspire and spice up your bond.

If you are single and looking to welcome a partner into your life, then use the energy of pairs to attract a partner. Make sure the bed is big enough for two, leave room in closets and drawers for a partner's stuff to rest, and use symbols, artwork and décor to visualize the partner you're attracting. If you're single and prefer to be that way, the bedroom is a place to build a powerful statement about you and your love and care of yourself.

Bed placement

Placing the bed where the Chi flows best in the room is very important. Once again, a sleeping state is when we are most energetically influenced by hidden forces. It's best if the bed can be placed so that the sleeper is in the command position: with a solid wall behind the headboard and a clear view of the doorway, without being in a direct line with the door.

Chi will naturally flow into a room from the doorway and then search for the closest exit out, usually through a window. It's best not to be in direct line with this Chi flowing into the room because it can be too impactful on a sleeping soul. It's also best not to be under a window where the Chi is flowing out because some of your vital Chi might be pulled out with it.

Often, it's impossible to place the bed in the ideal Feng Shui location for your bedroom. It's a challenge especially in older homes that have multiple windows, heating units and other obstacles for furniture placement. If this is your situation, consider how you can best protect the sleeper from harsh Chi flow or from losing vital chi. Sometimes simple fixes can deflect and circulate the Chi so it is less harmful. Patterned bedcovers, lighting, vibrant artwork, heavy drapes or a hanging crystal are some things you can use to redirect the energetic flow so the bed is kept in a supportive Chi flow.

© Jill O'Connor

See your bedroom from a new perspective

Have you ever sat in your bed and just looked around the room? Try it and notice what you see and how you feel. Is there anything distracting or noticeably annoying? Consider your bedding, window treatments and other furnishings in the room. Are these items that encourage a warm and sensuous nest? What about your artwork and décor? Does it support a peaceful retreat and encourage romance? What kind of energy is surrounding the room and surrounding you while you're in there? Is the room too hot? Too cold? Too noisy? Too bright or too dim? Do you notice uncomfortable drafts or unpleasant stuffiness? What about your bed ... is it comfortable or not? Is the bedding cozy or scratchy? Do the window coverings allow in the amount of light and air that you and your partner prefer? What kind of distractions do you notice in the room? Are there piles of clutter, work to be done, laundry to be folded? Are there electronic distractions and electromagnetic fields near the sleeping space? Notice it and remedy what you can.

Under the bed

Don't forget to look under your bed. Ideally air and fresh Chi should be able to circulate over and under you as you sleep – items stored under the bed stop this nourishing flow and can contribute to sleeplessness and health issues. Remember that everything has its own energy, and that energy interacts with our own personal energy. This interaction is most dramatic when we're in an unconscious and vulnerable state like sleep. Clear out whatever is stored under the bed and you will sleep better. I've had countless clients who were suffering from sleep challenges and were amazed at how much better they slept when they moved these objects with activating energy out from under the bed and preferably out of the room entirely. I've had clients find old journals, bills, legal documents and even copies of their divorce papers under the bed! These items are all very emotionally charged items to be sleeping on!!

Who and what is invited in?

It's amazing what things (and thus what types of energy) people allow into their bedrooms. I've seen it all ... financial paperwork, weapons, art supplies from a stifled hobby, clothes that don't fit but are kept "just in case", trash and dishes, pictures of family members, piles of laundry, electronics and much more. Imagine the powerful energy of these items nearby while you are in a dream state and your energy is most freely interacting with the energy of the space around you. No wonder people have difficulty sleeping or feel unrested when they wake up! The bedroom is such a critical space for your health and happiness, be sure to choose what you place in it wisely and deliberately! Consider the energetic impact of everything you place in this space and make sure it deliberately supports rest and connection.

I remember working with a friend on the Feng Shui in her new home. She had recently married and was combining possessions and space with her new husband. We were talking about her bedroom and how to set it up supportively for both of them. Her husband was from a military background and had lots of memorabilia from his career. One item he cherished was a model of a Blackhawk helicopter. It had always been in his bachelor bedroom and so he automatically moved it into their new bedroom. To him it was a symbol of strength and spirit, but to her it represented war and unrest. In her mind it was not something that was going to encourage rest and romance! Ultimately we decided to encourage her husband to move the piece to a space where its energy could be honored without impacting such a sacred space like the bedroom.

Guest rooms

The same thoughts apply with guest rooms as with bedrooms. The one thing I run into often is an empty dedicated guest room, while other spaces and areas of life are crowed together. If you only use your guest room a couple of times a year then consider whether other parts of your life could spread into that area and alleviate pressure elsewhere in the house -- could the room be better suited as an office, a toy room, an exercise room, or even a closet? Food for thought.

The bedroom is the one space where I discourage pictures of friends or family. I always remind clients that hanging a picture of someone is like energetically inviting them into the space! Remember that this is your private and romantic space. It's the one place you should be able to retreat from the pressures of the outside world, including any children, meddling family members, or nosy friends! There are no pictures of our kids in our bedroom, but just outside our bedroom door I've hung some of my favorites of them so they are always the first and last thing I see every day! My kids get our attention all day long while myself, my husband, and our relationship get put on the backburner. Keeping pictures of them out the room is one way to create a boundary and create space for just us for a change.

As a reminder, televisions, laptops, and smartphones are all devices that distract our attention from our present space and company. And even more so, these devices can allow others, even strangers into our most private space. That's another important reason to be wary of the kind of energy you invite in!

Summary

In today's busy world it's critical to carve out a private space for rest and connection. Bedrooms can become a peaceful or romantic sanctuary with a few Feng Shui considerations. Bed placement, enhancements to encourage connection and a deliberate choice of what is allowed into the room will create a quick shift for the better in this space.

16 Work Spaces

~ Expression of Creative Energy ~

~ Related to Our Accomplishments ~

~ Goals ~ Successes ~

No matter what your occupation or course of study is, whether you are a student, an artist, a chef, a secretary, a mechanic, an executive, or work in any other profession, your work space should symbolize and support what you want to accomplish in the space.

Ideally, the area should be dedicated to the work at hand, functional, supportive, inspiring, and energizing so that you are easily able to do the job.

This section applies to a home office, study space, or any kind of work space that you have in your home. This is where you pursue your goals and express your creative energy. If your profession is a chef, then the kitchen is your workspace. If you're a mechanic, then the garage is your creative workspace. Perhaps you're a scientist and a lab is where you create. Apply these ideas to any space where you pursue your career and passion, a business setting, a student workspace, a cubicle, or an artistic studio space for art, dance, or music.

Creating space for your passion and work

Any pursuit or passion needs space to be expressed. I've been in enough guest rooms/home offices, playrooms/home studio spaces, and dining rooms/study spaces to know that it's a challenge to create a dedicated space for your pursuits in a home setting. However, creating a space that is specialized assures more support and success for your interests. A space that holds all the tools of your trade, functional space to work, and energetic inspiration will streamline your creative process allowing more energy to be spent where it counts. When you create a separate place to work, you give yourself permission to focus on one thing at a time, and that is why it is so powerful to have a dedicated workspace where you can pursue your passion. In an ideal world, the work you do is your passion!

If you don't have a dedicated workspace you can face unnecessary challenges. You can set up in the kitchen for the day but then get distracted by household chores. Sit down in the living room to do a project, and suddenly the TV, conversations, or other family activities begin to interfere. You can waste countless minutes looking for misplaced items that don't have a home of their own, addressing tasks and people that aren't work related, and setting up and breaking down your area. With no physical boundaries around the work, the boundaries around the various roles of life can become very blurry! Most people find that their work suffers because the space they work in is ungrounded, inefficient, and distracting. They end up finding their work situation frustrating, and worst of all, unsatisfying. That is certainly not the kind of energy anyone wants to put into their creative pursuits! Although freeing up space to create a dedicated work space can be a challenge, the benefits can make it very worthwhile.

Whatever your work or your passion, define a space where you can pursue it. Give your dreams physical room to grow by creating a space for the creative expression you seek. Once you've defined the workspace, consciously arrange and design it to support your creative flow. Once again the energy and love that you've put into the space for your pursuits will contribute to efficient and productive work flow, less stress and strain, and more inspired and creative results.

Clutter in the work space verses creative messes!

Clutter presents many challenges in any space, but in the workspace it can signify distractions and creative blocks. You want to sit down to do some work but first you need to clear a space or find the right tools to begin with. Clutter can result in wasted time, stress and hindered production, and often is a sign of delayed decisions or procrastination. Too much stuff in your field of view can muddle the mind and creates chaos and confusion.

As with other rooms, do your best to keep the work space neat and clutter free. Fill the space with things that you love, only what you need to use for your work, and items that keep you focused on your goals. Keep these items as neat and organized as possible by giving everything a home and taking time to put things away when not in use.

Of course, workspaces often get messy in the course of the creative process. Piles and disorder can be a simple sign of a project in progress. People have different work styles and sometimes the chaos is par for the course. It might look like clutter to others but often there is a method to the madness! As long as everything in the mix is needed, useful and inspirational to the activity then it is not really clutter. Be honest about what you need in the space. Consciously consider if what you're keeping and how you're keeping it is helping or hindering your progress.

Arranged for success

One of the most important things you can do to support yourself and your work is to set your workspace up so that you are in "the command position." This means that you have a solid wall behind you and a good view of the room in front of you and especially of the door. Symbolically, being in the command position puts us in charge of the work that we do. It gives us a view over all that is being created, and prevents someone from going behind our back at work. In work, as in all of our creative endeavors, we want to be in the spot that gives us the best possible advantage.

Setting up in the command position generally requires a bit more space, so it is often disregarded in office design. More often than not I see workstations facing the wall with the workers back exposed to the open room. Whenever there is an option for changing it, I encourage rearranging the space for a trial period. People are amazed by how much better they feel all around when they have positioned themselves in the more influential spot. Subliminally, our central nervous systems are much more sensitive than we're aware of. Making this one change to the space can initiate an unexpected and potent sense of physical and emotional ease. This is a small but significant change that has a big impact on all aspects of how you work.

Try all the options

Take a minute and try this exercise: Sit with your back to the door for a while, then try sitting facing the door. Now put a desk between you and the door you're facing. See if you can notice differences in your sense of "ease" in each position. I always prefer to be able to see the door wherever I land.

If setting up your work station in the command position is not an option, then consider placing a mirror on the wall in front of you so you can see anything that's approaching you in the mirror. This really works in creating a sense of ease about what is behind you.

You can also place a screen, plant, or table of some sort behind you to provide a further energetic shield from the open space at your back.

Once you've finalized where your workspace will be, make sure you have sufficient room, consistent storage, and good lighting for the task at hand. Workspaces tend to be brighter and have more overall yang energy than some other home spaces. This is because we need to draw on that energy for our creative expressions. Choose furnishings and work tools that are safe, comfortable, and pleasing. Last, make sure you have space for all the tools of your trade close at hand.

Supportive symbols

Last, but definitely not least, enhance your workspace and/or the room with colors that energize the space, and artwork/symbols that inspire you and your work. Ideally whatever you are looking at while seated at your desk pleases and uplifts you, while at the same time keeps you focused.

One client I worked with was an attorney that was studying for the bar exam in a new state. They wanted to set up a dedicated study space at home. Since their dining room wasn't used often we converted it to a temporary study area. The room had great windows to let light in, a large table sufficient to spread out all the reference materials, and convenient shelves for other supplies too. First, we made sure that she was seated in the command position at the table, added lighting, and set up her computer and printer so she could access them easily. Finally, we talked about adding some symbolic décor pieces into the space that would continue to inspire her studies and keep her focused on the goal of passing the bar. All of this served to keep her focused on the goal at hand and support her with all she needed while pursuing her studies.

Use the Bagua Map

You can enhance your work space even further by applying the Bagua Map to this individual workroom and to your desk space. Lay the map from the entrance to the room and also from where you sit at the desk. Then add enhancements to each corner of the room and to each part of the desk in any specific area that needs enhancing. For example, if you wanted to encourage wealth and abundance in your work life, you would add symbols of wealth and prosperity to the far left corner of the work room, and to the far left corner of the desk. Of course, this can be done in any room corresponding to any life area, but I remind you of it here because I most often see it being needed in relation to work and creative activities.

17 Passageways

~ Chi Passages in the Space ~

~ Similar to Veins and Arteries or Roadways and Waterways ~

> Hallways allow Chi to flow from one area to another. Staircases allow Chi to flow between floors. Both the design and décor of these features affects the way that Chi flows, sometimes beneficially, sometimes detrimentally.
>
> Ideally, these passageways provide a clear direction for people and Chi to flow through at a safe and beneficial pace. Energy should be able to move from one space to another, nourishing all areas that extend from these passageways.

Hallways

Hallways are passageways allowing Chi to move through a space. They are similar to highways that allow cars to rapidly bypass more congested areas, or to arteries in the body that rush nutrients to distant destinations. Hallways allow the Chi to travel quickly and directly. The flow of Chi is altered as it enters a long and narrow corridor, tending to speed up and whip towards the end. This flow can be detrimental to things or spaces at the end, and at the same time can deplete Chi from rooms to the sides because it is speeding by too fast to turn in.

The narrower the passageway, the more the speed of the energy is amplified through a space. If the energy is being conducted too quickly then opportunities, money, and potential relationships don't stick around. The Feng Shui goal for hallways is to slow the Chi down so that it is not doing damage, and so that it has time to equally nourish the spaces on either side.

On the other hand, if a length is cluttered, the Chi can't flow effectively at all. It is slowed too much to energize spaces at either side or the end of the pathway. In this case clutter can act like a blockage. If hallways are like arteries for chi, then cluttered hallways can be like cholesterol filled blood vessels. Instead of the ideal meandering flow, this flow is unhealthy because it is slow, stagnant, and not vital.

When correcting the Chi flow here, it's important to consider what is located at the end. A long narrow corridor leading to a back entrance simply speeds up the energy and then dumps it back outside of your house. If you have a bathroom at the end the Chi is encouraged right down the drains. Again, vital life Chi is allowed out before it has a chance to feed the home. If a bedroom is located down the hall, the occupant of the bedroom could be adversely affected by the negative energy flow. It's important to appropriately redirect the flow of energy so its nourishing benefit can be felt and held onto before it gets to these destinations.

Ideally, hallways should be open or at least feel open, to allow easy movement and to provide a clear direction of where to go. You want the energy to get where it needs to go, but not too quickly. The flow can often be shifted simply by taking the attention off of the end or destination and slowing and/or redirecting it by drawing the attention side to side instead. Chi can be gently sidetracked and slowed down by placing a patterned carpet on the floor, or using mirrors, artwork, and lighting on the side walls to call your attention laterally across the space. Hanging enhancements such as wind chimes or faceted crystals from the ceiling also help lift and circulate the Chi as it travels through the space.

Often, passageways can tend to feel long, narrow, and dark. Correct this with lighting from above and also from the sides. Light coming in from other rooms encourages a feeling of wideness. This can be accomplished with sconces on the side walls, open doorways, or glass doors that allow light in from side rooms.

Summary

Correcting for how the Chi flows through hallways and passageways in a house can be very powerful in keeping vital Chi in the space long enough to energize various parts of your life. If you are feeling drained or rushed, or facing health complications related to blood flow, consider looking at how the energy is flowing (or not) through your homes hallways.

Staircases

Staircases play a critical role in how the Chi flows in your environment and from one level of a space to another. If you visualize Chi being like water flowing through your space, then staircases instantly seem to become "waterfalls" where most of the Chi flows in a downward direction rapidly.

In Feng Shui, we look at where that waterfall of vital Chi is going. It is hitting a dead end and causing the Chi to stagnate? Is it rushing out the door at the bottom of the stairs and taking all of its vital benefit with it? Is it rushing into the baby's nursery and creating an unrestful space there?

Just as in a hallway, the goal of Feng Shui is to slow the flow of Chi down and direct it so it isn't harshly affecting anything at the bottom of the stairs or flowing out of the space! There are many ways to lift and divert the Chi flow of your steps to create positive results.

© Sarah Commerford

Adding a light fixture above the stairs lifts the attention up. A decorative fixture, like a chandelier, is encouraged. If lighting is unimpressive you can also hang a decorative mobile or a faceted crystal above the stairway to "lift" the energy.

Artwork or photographs can be placed in a way that raises the chi. I often see pictures hung in a slanted or stepping stone fashion on stairways. As you go up the stairs the pictures go up to. As you descend the stairs the images descend right beside you. This positioning enhances and encourages the downward flow of energy. In fact we want to downplay and discourage that flow.

Instead, place artwork pictures straight across the stairway wall, so that all images are at the same level. This trick helps to slow the downward flow of energy and encourage it to stick around rather than rush down and out.

It's also great to consider the energy of the artwork you choose to place around a staircase. Choose artwork with upward flowing energy.

Images of trees that grow upward, mountains that point upward or images that encourage upward energy (like hot air balloons floating or birds flying) are more good ways to correct the down flow.

You can also place things on the steps or at the bottom of the flight to divert the current. Place plants at the bottom or along the treads to add more "upward" energy to the stairs. Use a carpet runner with a busy and winding pattern, or place a decorative area rug at the base of the stairs. Lately I've seen fun decorative accents on the stair risers including painting each riser a different color, and painting a design or an inspirational message on it that can be enjoyed as you walk up the stairs. I've even seen stair risers painted to look like book ends with favorite book titles. What a fun way to divert attention and shift the energy to a playful or inspired vibe.

There are ways to correct for wherever the Chi is flowing too. If your front door is directly at the base of your main staircase, it is best to make sure the door is solid with few windows to make it harder for the Chi to escape. If there are windows, consider covering them with curtains or place decorative crystals, sun catchers, or stained glass in the window. Hang something sturdy and decorative on the door/wall at the bottom of the stairs to slow or redirect the chi. A mirror can also be hung on the back of the door to reflect Chi back into the space.

One corporate client I worked with had a large spiral staircase in the center of their office space. At the top of the stairs was the Assistant to the General Manager's desk, and just behind that the doorway leading into the General Manager's office. Not far from the bottom of the stairs there were several staff desks that sat between the staircase and the main entrance. The staff member upstairs felt depleted and somewhat powerless in her role. Her energy was effectively being dragged down the stairs daily. The staff members at the bottom of the stairs consistently felt harried. They were being bombarded by the energy flowing from the large staircase. Aside from moving staff desks slightly, we also added some corrections to the staircase, like plants and artwork to redirect the Chi and better support everyone in the space.

Summary

These are all simple suggestions that make a big difference in how Chi flows in your house and most importantly, to different areas of your life. The good news is that you can redirect and send Chi to areas that need revitalizing by using many of these tips.

18 Kid's Spaces

~ Creative Expression ~ Growth ~

~ Expansion ~ Innocence ~ Potential ~

Many of the ideas in the book apply to childrens' areas as well. However, babies and children are especially sensitive to the energies that surround them and how they are flowing, so taking extra care in arranging the rooms they spend lots of time in is encouraged. In addition, when adults are arranging or Feng Shui-ing a child's space, it's easy to forget what things look like and feel like from a child's viewpoint. This section addresses this and more with special notes that apply just to childrens' spaces.

Nurseries and childrens' bedrooms

It's recommended that babies get fourteen or more hours of rest each day so that they can grow and learn. Less sleep is needed as they get older, but the time that youngsters spend in their room, whether playing or sleeping, can have a strong effect on their behavior, school results, health, sleep habits, and creativity. After working in this field for so many years, I truly believe that children benefit in many ways from the extra attention to energy flow that is put into planning their rooms.

Most people consider the aesthetics of their child's room as they set it up for them, but overlook the effect of unseen energies on the kids. If you create a supportive room with good Chi flow, you will be setting your child up to have good energy. They will be happy, rested, and have better behavior because they are so supported while in this quiet state. Everyone else will be better rested too! If you overlook these factors, you can be setting your children up to be consistently tired, cranky, and ultimately less healthy, which affects the rest of the family too.

> Sleep, rest and rejuvenation are the essential purposes of nurseries and children's bedrooms.
>
> Creating a room that supports this with good energy flow has a huge impact on a young one's growth, health, learning, and temperament.
>
> Ideally the room is safe, comforting, quiet, and softly lit, all to encourage quiet, rest, and sleep.

For nurseries and kid's bedrooms, try to start with a clean slate. Take everything out. Clean the room thoroughly. Open up the doors and windows in the room to let fresh air flow in. Next, do an energetic space clearing and bless the space with positive intentions. You can read more about this sacred process in the section about Space Clearing in Chapter 9. In many ways, youngsters are defenseless against lingering energy that has attached itself to a room or objects in a room, so clearing this out first can be powerful.

When choosing colors for the room, remember that color is energy, and every color has a different vibration that is closely related to different moods and emotions. Color can be stimulating or calming. Children are more sensitive to these differing wavelengths of energy, so be aware of this as you choose colors. For paint, linens, and artwork in a space that is predominately for sleeping, look for soft, calm colors in neutrals or pastels. Bright colors, like hot pink or royal blue are too stimulating for a young child when present in excess. Instead, add pops of bright color for interest in accents like pillows and pictures in the space.

Hidden blessings

If you're planning to paint the space, consider writing special blessings for your child on the wall (in pencil!) before painting. We did this with both of our daughter's rooms when we were setting the space up as their nurseries. We wrote words such as "loved, empowered, joyful, supported, playful, artistic, laughter, healthy" all over the walls and then painted over it. It was a fun and powerful process that positively set the energy imprint of the room.

To arrange the room, start by placing the crib or bed in a command position. The goal is for the child to see the entrance door and as much of the room as possible. Ideally the bed is placed away from windows and away from electrical outlets and vents, too. It can be challenging to find a wall or corner that meets all of these needs in modern homes, but look for the best possible option. If you're unsure of the best location, try all the options. Really try it for yourself. Place the bed. Lie down in the bed. Look around and notice what you can see, what you can feel. Perhaps even sleep in the space for a night or two. Trust your intuition and choose the best option. Then watch your child's response over time and adjust as needed.

Room arrangement could be a cure

If you have an infant or young child that is having health issues, behavioral issues, or simply isn't sleeping well, take a look at their bedroom. If your child is consistently coming into your bedroom to sleep at night, they are not only looking for comfort from you, it's a sure sign that they don't find their room comfortable to be in. I talk to many parents who have children sleeping with them all night or have "little visitors" throughout the night. Considering the room arrangement is hardly ever something they think of to solve the problem but it's often just the solution. Check their space for challenges! Be persistent in making adjustments. You may have to tweak things a few times until it gets better. Taking the time to remedy any invisible energetic impacts will be worth it when everyone is sleeping and happy again. Trust me – I've lived it!

Use all of your senses when testing out the space. Pay attention to uncomfortable drafts, unpleasant smells, or distant noises. In one child's bedroom everything seemed fine, but once on the bed you could hear and feel a vibration coming from a fan in the attic. It was set to turn on when the attic space got too hot. Whenever it kicked on the child would be startled awake but no one could figure out why his sleep was so disturbed. It was a quick fix to turn off the fan at night and everyone was able to sleep better. Another parent discovered that a stuffed animal placed on the bureau threw a frightening looking shadow above the bed at night that was quite unsettling. It moved to a new location and her child was more at ease.

To keep the room focused on quiet rest and sleep, arrange differing levels of lighting so that you can lower the lighting at bedtime. Choose window coverings that sufficiently block the light to further enhance a restful experience. When choosing what to bring in for accents, consider all five of the senses: Notice what your child sees as they drift off to sleep and groggily wakes up in the morning. Make sure they have a positive view. Choose artwork that is calming and supportive. Choose fabrics that are soft and inviting, and add a variety of textures through the space to encourage exploration. Soft music or white noise may be appropriate and will help drown out other household noises. Finally, consider using aromatherapy in the space to further support a calming atmosphere. Diffusing a few drops of lavender or chamomile in the room will add to its appeal and help relax little ones as they fall off to sleep. You can find more information about using aromatherapy in Chapter 6.

Last, but certainly not least, only put things into the room that will encourage rest or quiet time. Overall, the bedroom should be simple. In effect, a visual resting space to encourage the rest and concentration that is needed. Besides sleep, this room is a space that can give children much needed time to play quietly, reflect on things and recharge their body and mind. A few books, stuffed animals, quiet dolls, coloring or journaling supplies are appropriately quiet for the space. Reserve all of the noisy and interactive toys for more active living and play spaces where stimulating experiences are encouraged. Loud noises, bright colors, activating toys, televisions and computers, large mirrors, and things like aquariums or fountains are not suited for this space. Keep clutter to a minimum in the bedroom. Not only will it be easier to maintain but it will be much more supportive for the child.

It's best to keep electrical appliances as far away from the bed as possible. Electrical outlets, alarm clocks, radios, cell phones, and light fixtures all circulate an invisible energy fields around them. In simple terms these items can interfere with our own natural energy flow. Children tend to be even more sensitive to that, so it's especially important to keep these electrical objects to a minimum. When they are necessary, keep them as far away from the bed as possible.

Remember, too, that you can apply the Bagua Map to the individual room and specifically enhance the nine life areas for your child's benefit. Encourage strong family relationships by placing a positive family picture in the Family Gua. Set them up for success in their studies with enhancements in the Knowledge Gua. Honor their accomplishments by highlighting awards they've earned in the Recognition Gua. Using the Bagua Map is another way to intentionally honor and energize these life areas for your child. You can find more information about how to apply the Bagua Map to a space in Chapter 5.

As children get older, they want to have more input into what their room looks and feels like. Let them into the design process but provide gentle guidance. Allow them to express themselves, while also inspiring them to become aware of energy flow and how it affects them. Explain how a cluttered room affects their focus and vitality. Teach them to consider the energy of the stuff they keep. Explain how using technology in their bedrooms affects sleep. (Instead provide a space where they can use technology without interfering with rest.) Ideally, a child can express their interests and still balance their space with positive and strong images, such as a happy family picture, awards, powerful sayings, religious items, accomplishments or projects. Hopefully, they'll see the difference between filling their room with positive versus negative inspirations. Best, they will be empowered with this information for life!

Playrooms

If you are lucky enough to have a dedicated play space for kids, it's best to arrange the room with their energy in mind. This is a space where loud toys, televisions, video games, reading and art materials, board games, and more are all finally welcome. It's a room where friends and family can come together to share in the fun.

> Playrooms, on the other hand are a more yang space where kids can let loose to connect with themselves, their imagination, their friends and their skills. The energy of this space will likely be more pumped up than other rooms. Good lighting, bright and fun colors, and uplifting artwork that reflect the children's energy and personality is best for this type of space.

When arranging a playroom, think safety first, softening edges and securing things to the wall so bouncing and rambunctiousness can happen without injury. Since playrooms are spaces that can become messy easily, look for storage solutions that are easy for children to use. Keep the energy of the room fresh and clutter free by purging regularly. Let go of anything that they've outgrown and make sure you only keep a manageable amount of toys. How many sets of dishes does the play kitchen need? How many different dolls/cars/trucks can they play with at one time? How many markers and crayons are needed on a daily basis? It's great if you can keep some of their toys and activities stored away and then periodically switch things out so they get fresh new items to play with every once in a while. I love doing this with my kids – it's like Christmas day again every time we do it!

Let kids help decide how their spaces should be organized and decorated. This can be a very empowering and inspiring space for kids, especially if they can help create a space that supports them. Let them select colors, and choose which toys to keep. Let them choose, or even better, create the artwork in the room. This should be a space where kids are free to be kids, so let the arrangement and décor reflect that.

Study spaces

Study spaces, whether dedicated space, in the bedroom or part of a living or play space, can be arranged to encourage focus, creativity and good grades! I've seen a variety of kids' study spaces in my work, with everything from a desk in the corner of the bedroom, the kitchen table, the living room floor, or even the bed being used as a work space. Everyone has different space available and different preferences in how they like to work. However, providing a focused task area and arranging it mindfully can benefit children's achievement greatly.

Having to clear a space for homework and projects each time creates unnecessary struggle right up front, so start by creating a comfortable task space. Make sure the area has good lighting so nothing gets missed. Choose a quiet location with minimal distraction so the student can stay focused on the task at hand. Keep all the required tools to succeed handy so there's no need to search out pens, scissors, or calculators instead of working. Ideally, set up the workspace so the student is in the command position, or give them the best view of the room possible, so they can be in command of their studies. Finally, enhance the workspace with visual encouragements of study goals and inspirational reminders that keep them focused.

If you have a child that is challenged at school or struggles with any subject, take a look at the space where they do their work and make positive changes to it. Providing a space that supports what they need to accomplish and inspires them in their work is worth a try.

Summary

I've seen Feng Shui help kids sleep better, be better students, and alleviate stress and behavioral issues! By paying attention to the unseen energy that surrounds our children, and harnessing it so it's positive, and supportive, we can help our children thrive!

19 Bathrooms and Laundry Rooms

~ Cleansing ~ Release ~ Rejuvenation ~

~ Renewal ~ Wealth ~

Bathrooms are spaces that are designed for the purpose of cleansing and washing away dirt and toxins from our bodies. In effect, these spaces are very much related to the process of releasing anything that you or your body doesn't need any more. What seems like a basic daily function can actually be symbolic of a much more potent process of release.

In addition, according to Feng Shui, flowing water is symbolic of flowing money and wealth. Ideally, bathrooms are elementally balanced, with corrections made to prevent the loss of vital chi.

Down the drain

Bathrooms have an abundance of water sources, including toilets, sink faucets, and shower heads, making this space very symbolic of wealth. But, bathrooms naturally have downward flowing energy, with the water flowing into the basin and swiftly down the drain. Although we want the water flow to effectively remove dirt and toxins from our bodies, we do not want our vital Chi and financial resources to flow down the drains along with the cleansed stuff. Without planning, this is exactly what happens in this space. The natural flow of Chi seeks out the exit. In Feng Shui, we want to do everything we can to move the waste out while keeping the healthy fresh Chi (and wealth) in, to nourish the family. There are many quick and easy things that can be done to counter this negative flow and keep the good stuff around.

© Kerri Miller

First, make sure the bathroom plumbing is in good working order. Leaky pipes let all that Chi drip away and over time can make residents feel constantly "drained." Clogged pipes are another problem, not allowing the toxins to be carried away properly and creating a thick heavy stuck-ness in the energy of the space. This is a critical area to make sure is in good working order because it is so closely related to health, hygiene and flowing money!

Raising and circulating the Chi

Make sure your bathroom has sufficient lighting. Light lifts and brightens the energy in any space. It's a very positive cure for this space in particular because the light helps counteract the downward flow. In addition, make sure this space is clean and clutter free. Keeping the space clean is of course important in terms of sanitation. Keeping it clutter free will help keep the energy of the space "up" as well. Make it a point to regularly check the bathroom closets, cabinets, and drawers. It's easy for half used bottles of shampoo and other toiletries, and bottles of expired medications to build up and clutter up this space. Use what you keep in there regularly, purge what you don't use, and try to keep some open and available space in all of these nooks so that the energy has room to flow and not get stuck amongst all the clutter.

One of the best ways to prevent a drain of vital Chi via the bathroom is to keep the bathroom door closed. That way vital Chi flowing into the house will pass by the bathroom and move on to energize other important spaces like the kitchens and bedrooms. Keeping the bathroom drains closed when not in use and the toilet lid closed, are also important ways to slow vital Chi down so that it doesn't leave before benefitting the space/occupants first.

Other ways to stabilize the sinking energy of the bathroom is to lift the energy by placing plants or images of plants in the space. Plants naturally grow upward and offset the obvious downward flow. A faceted glass crystal can also be hung from the ceiling to lift and circulate the energy in the space. Consider paint colors, fabrics and inspiring artwork to keep things flowing in a positive way.

Although bathrooms seem like a purely functional space, they are powerful in releasing what we don't want as well as rejuvenating our health and well-being. Extra touches to make the bathroom a sacred space where these daily rituals can take place is a bonus to the health and vitality of the whole home and to the occupants too. Special touches like luxurious wash towels, candles and aromatherapy not only help to revitalize the occupants but send a symbolic message about what is important back out to the energy of the entire residence. The more uplifting this space is to you and all who enter, the less likely the energy will rush away.

Finally, consider where your bathrooms fall within the Bagua Map of your home. In most cases, you won't be able to relocate a bathroom, but by being aware of where it falls in your space and which life area it falls into can make your more empowered in countering negative effects in that area.

Laundry rooms

Laundry rooms are similar to bathrooms due to the downward draining energy of these large appliances. The same cures apply in this space to raise and circulate the chi. And while you're at it, consider the overall energy of this space. Just because it's only a workspace doesn't mean that it can't be uplifting and inspiring at the same time. Consider paints, artwork, organizational storage, and workspace functionality to help boost the energy of this space and make the work you do in there more pleasing.

Summary

Being aware of the kind of energy rooms like bathrooms have within your house is important. It allows you to counteract negative energy flows and balance them, making the space feel better and giving you an advantage.

20 Closets

~ Subconscious ~ Secrets We Keep ~

~ Hidden Feelings About Yourself ~

~ Reflection of Your Self Esteem ~

Symbolically, closets correspond to the subconscious part of our mind. They are a reflection of the secrets we keep and the feelings we have about ourselves. Even if the closet if closed and hiding the contents, it still has a subliminal impact on us. Ideally, closets are well lit, organized, and appealing to look at and get stuff from.

Closets tend to be the place where we throw everything that we don't want others to see. Think of that moment when you've had unexpected company arrive, and you run around gathering up piles of stuff from around the house and then hide it in the closets! We're afraid to let people in on the secret that our daily lives are a little messy, so we hide it away.

Our personal clothing closets are also a strong representation of our own self esteem. How we are maintaining the closet and the items in the closet is a direct reflection of how we are maintaining ourselves.

Overstuffed, unorganized closets can manifest as overwhelm and confusion in your thoughts and actions. They can result in time lost looking for items, unhappy feelings and guilt about how we look and how we're keeping things, and overall frustration. Think about this - every morning you step into a dark closet, look inside and rifle through clothes that you don't like, and don't fit, trip on things that are dropped on the floor, grab what you need, then shut the door and run! That is the energy you are setting yourself up for during the whole day! Now consider opening the door, turning on appropriate lighting, seeing a wall of organized clothes that you are inspired to wear and that makes you feel good. The floor is clear and there's plenty of room to move things around. Now you're starting your day much differently!

What is in your clothes closet?

When you open the door to get dressed in the morning do you love the choices in front of you? Are you choosing from pieces that authentically represent who you are now, or looking at clothes that fit and reflect the person that you were in the past? Keep in mind that your daily energy is affected when you are keeping/wearing items that "aren't you", that you don't like, or that don't fit.

Like it or not your closet has a major impact on your overall energy. Maintaining your closet so that it is full of useful things you love and it's easy to find what you need, has the ability to shift the energy of your life every single morning. This one act can change the quality of your daily life just by setting you up for a better morning. Finding all of your stuff quickly, feeling good in what you're wearing, and being able to get ready easily in the morning sets up your whole day to be happier, easier, and smoother! The one simple act of maintaining your closet will reflect a major shift in how you see yourself, how you are seen by others, and whether your day and your life flow with ease and grace or not.

Even though items in the closet are out of sight, they are definitely still not out of mind. Those closets, their contents and the way they are kept, neat or not, have a major impact on you, your space, and your energy even when you're away from them. You may not be able to see the mess and unwanted items, but they are still having an impact on how peaceful (or not!) your inner world is. That stuff still has an energy that affects you and subliminally you will always be "hearing" and aware of the disorder. It's best to take on the project and shift this space as soon as you can.

Start by correcting the lighting in the space. Consider painting the walls to brighten and freshen up the space. It may seem like lots of extra work for a closet, but now that you know that how you treat your closet is a reflection of how you're treating yourself, you should understand why taking the extra step is worth it.

Pull everything out of your closet and only put back things that you love, that reflect who you are today (or perhaps who you are striving to be), and things that fit comfortably and look good. Have a friend or loved one help you choose what to keep. Most of us only truly wear one tenth of what's in our closet. Commit to moving the other stuff on and make room for being who you really are. Ideally, when you're done clearing you'll have at least 20% empty space in the closet (more is better!). This allows your clothes to hang freely without getting wrinkled and also gives you room to grow without cramming things in again. Once you've purged, take time to organize what is left so that it's easy to find what you need.

Last, add some extra enhancements to the space. If you have room, hang a pretty picture or a crystal. Take time to add some scented sachets in your drawers or spray a pleasant scented mist in the space. These extra steps are equivalent to nurturing self-care touches that we all benefit from.

Facing the mess in the closet can be daunting, but the results will be well worth the effort. Figure out a plan that works best for you to tackle the project. For some, dedicating a weekend to the task is best. Others may benefit from committing to clearing out three to five items each day. Some Personal Organizers suggest that you tackle the whole category of clothing at one time – pulling it all out from wherever it is stored and putting it all in one place to work through. In effect this lets you see how much you have (too much?) and is further encouragement to help you pare it down. However, you accomplish sorting through your clothing storage, you'll surely get some positive energy flowing while making more room for living your authentic life.

All of the above guidelines apply to other types of closets in the house too. Even though a linen closet doesn't contain clothes that affect your self-esteem, the way that the closet is kept is still a valuable reflection. Whether you're storing paper supplies, linens, coats and shoes or toiletries, be sure to keep only what is pertinent and useful. Leave some open space in the closet so that you can easily put new stock away when you come home from the store or have guests who need to hang up coats. And of course there is no reason why you can't make all of these spaces look more beautiful and appealing by using good lighting, color, baskets, and more.

Summary

It's worth it to shed some light on the way you take care of things that are normally out of sight. Treat these items with as much regard as every other part of your home and you'll have a better command of your inner and outer worlds. When these private spaces are in order it releases blocks and invites ease into your life.

21 The Attic

~ Higher Ambitions ~ Goals ~ Wishes ~ Desires ~

In Feng Shui terms, attics symbolize our higher ambitions, goals, wishes and desires. Because it is above the main living space it also can represent "things hanging over our head" and can have an impact on the Chi flow of the entire house.

Ideally, the attic space is well lit, has clear access to everything, and the items in storage are organized. If the attic has been converted to a functional room, the space should be clutter free, uplifting and used regularly.

I'll deal with that later

If you think of your home like a human body that is standing up, then the attic parallels the head of the body. (The torso corresponds to the heart of the home, and the feet and legs correspond to the basement or foundation.) Having an attic full of random mixed up and disorganized stuff is like having a head full of random mixed up thoughts. If your attic is cluttered with items that aren't serving you, then you may have a challenging time setting new goals and moving forward in life. Whatever is up there, whether seen or not, it's still impacting all your home's occupants' ability to thrive!

Because of its lack of proximity to the heart of the home, the attic tends to be a space that is not very well used, either as living space or storage space. When I've previously led Feng Shui work groups, I almost always hear a groan from the audience when we begin to talk about the need to give the attic some attention. This is a space where people traditionally dump stuff and then run as fast as they can back to the living quarters. Most people have a perpetual "I'll deal with that later" attitude about the attic. But with lots of encouragement, many have succeeded in gaining back the upper hand over their attic storage spaces. The benefits are too numerous to count.

Getting started in the attic can be a challenge. It's usually not well lit, and for many seasons during the year, it's not very temperate to be in either. Consider this when choosing a time to tackle this area. One trick is to get the energy flowing in the space before you even go in to work on it. For a day or two before you start the project, turn the lights on and keep them on. Open any doors/windows/vents to the space and leave them open. Set up a fan that stays on to the start circulating the Chi up there. You can also hang a crystal in the space to help lift and circulate the chi. After a day or two of this you won't be able to resist going up there to sort through everything. Remember to take plenty of breaks and pace yourself as you go through this space.

Summary

Commit a block of time to shedding some light in your attic, letting fresh Chi blow in, and sort through and discard anything that is holding you back from the future you want. Maybe you'll uncover some long forgotten treasures while you're up there. One workshop participant rallied the whole family to go through boxes in the attic. They purged tons of stuff they no longer needed and during the process found several savings bonds that they were able to cash in! Even if you don't find any hidden gems, I guarantee you'll gain a good dose of peace of mind and maybe a much clearer vision of your bright future.

22 The Basement

~ Foundation in Life ~ The Unconscious Mind ~

~ Deeply Rooted Thoughts ~ Suppressed Desires ~

In Feng Shui terms, basements are the foundation of your house and are, therefore, the foundation of your home's health and energy. Basements, and the things stored there, represent your personal foundation in life. It reflects things deeply rooted in the subconscious mind, and is symbolic of your past.

Cluttered and stagnant basements can equal being stuck in the past or being unable to move forward with what you truly desire in life.

Ideally, the basement is safe, well lit, well ventilated, useful, organized, and uplifting. Regardless of how the space is used, whether for storage, work, or living space, basements can still be enhanced with color, furnishings, art, and plants as appropriate. This will lift the energy of the lower level, and subsequently the whole house.

Dark, cold, and damp

The basement is very important to the overall energy of the home and the vitality of the occupants within. Usually basements are dark, damp, and stuffy. They are another place where it's easy to drop things and scurry back away. In New England, where I live, many antique houses have basements that are just dark rooms with dirt floors and stone walls. Often they house the laundry room and a handyman/workshop area and some storage, but are fit for little else. I've consulted in many a home where you have to walk halfway down a dark, steep, rickety staircase before blindly grabbing for the pull string for the light. Once you turn on the light all you see is stones and dirt. Can we say c-c-cold and creeeeeeeeepy!

In homes where the basement has been converted into usable living spaces, storage areas, or work spaces like the laundry and garage, the space can still be prone to darkness and dampness because of its below ground proximity. Usually, the darker and damper the space, is the less likely it is utilized to its full potential.

Sometimes making structural changes to dry and or stabilize the space can be big investments. But in Feng Shui terms, making these improvements can have a big impact on the overall health and well-being of the occupants, and can significantly impact the overall energy of the house. Give yourself the strongest foundation possible by focusing some time, money, and energy on the basement level of your home. The results will be well worth it.

Warming things up

Basements don't have to be dreary and unwelcoming. The more energized they are, the more they will help nourish the entire residence. Here are some thoughts on sprucing up the basement space, Feng Shui style:

First, correct any safety issues in the space, including shoring up staircases and beams. Mark any obstacles like low ceilings or uneven floors so that they can be moved around safely. Do your best to dry out the space with a dehumidifier and or portable fan or heater. These steps will improve the comfort of the space. Be sure to maintain these improvements – especially remember to drain the dehumidifier often to prevent stagnant water from collecting.

Paint is a simple addition that can make even the darkest of basements feel brighter, warmer, and safer. Even if you have a foundation made out of stones you can paint them and add lots of life to the space. Some versions of paint also help in keeping moisture out. Also consider painting the floor where possible, or adding floor coverings to soften the space. This could be something as simple as laying down plywood on a dirt floor or putting carpeting, tile, or linoleum on a cement floor. Any step you take will add warmth to the basement.

Good lighting is key to both safety and comfort in the basement. Most basements only have a few small windows, if any at all. Adding lighting is a way to brighten, enliven and warm the space. Plus, it adds a level of security and comfort when you need to go down into this space. If you have low ceilings in this area, then consider adding uplights (lights that sit close to the floor but point the light beam upward) to visually lift the ceiling. Remember to add lighting into the corners too. This is one area where a simple string of small white holiday lights can make a big impact.

If you do have windows in the basement, wash them thoroughly inside and out. It's easy to ignore this area when it comes to cleaning and upkeep. But make it a point to wash the windows occasionally. And while you're at it, open the windows and let some fresh air in too. This one act has the ability to shift the energy of the space drastically in just a short time!

Cleaning and clearing

It's easy for years of possessions to accumulate down in the basement and never get reviewed because no one wants to go down and go through it all. But just like in the attic, whatever is stored there still has an impact on you and various areas of life. If you haven't taken the time to go through the things you have stored in the basement recently, make a plan to do it. De-clutter this space by getting rid of anything that no longer serves you. Organize what's left, so that it's easy to find and easy to reach.

Many homes in my area have converted the basement into useable family space like a family room, play room, office, or work out room. It's great if the space can be used in these ways, but there's still a tendency for the area to be neglected. Make it a point to organize and freshen up these spaces regularly. No matter how the space is used, be sure to open all the door and windows and let some fresh Chi in there every so often. Take a walk through and check on things down there. Taking this one action regularly will truly help shift the energy in the entire space.

Basements can tend to feel low and heavy. This is because of their proximity to the ground and because of the weight of the structure above. As mentioned, paint and lighting can help lift and lighten this energy. Hanging faceted glass crystals are another way to raise and circulate the energy of the basement. Artwork is another way to enliven the Chi of a basement. Why not be inspired by beautiful paintings on the wall instead of being creeped out by gloom when you head down those basement stairs!

Clearing and arranging your basement is more than a one-day project; I encourage you to spend some time there today. At a minimum, add some lighting down there so that when you have time to return it will be well lit and easier to work in. I also mentioned turning on a fan in the space to start circulating some energy. If the weather is mild enough open as many windows and doors as you can – letting some fresh Chi in is always a plus even if you can't do any more. Clearing the energy of the space is really beneficial, especially in older properties that carry a deep history in their foundations.

Some clients I work with just dive in and tackle this space in a few days' time. Others find it easier to pace themselves by committing to spending a certain amount of time in the basement each day, or committing to going through a specific area or a specific number of boxes each day. Once it's done, it will feel like a huge accomplishment and your whole house will feel more supported for the changes you have made. Small steps will eventually equal big returns.

One last note is that rooms that are located directly above basements or garages can often feel cold and unwelcoming. Many times you will need to put extra warmth into the living spaces above the basement to help ground them, and warm them up. One recent client had a master bedroom that was located directly over a cold basement made of dirt floors and a stone foundation. Although the master bedroom was a modern addition above the basement, it still felt very cold. You could almost sense the open, drafty void below. In this particular case we talked about using warm colors, thick and darker area rugs and carpeting, and denser fabrics in the bedroom to bring more warmth and coziness into this room above.

Summary

Remember that heat rises and if you pay some attention to the basement of your home, giving it some love and adding warmth, you'll feel benefits through the entire structure.

23 The Garage

~ Storage Space for Prized Possessions ~

~ Last and First Space You See When Coming or Going Home ~

> The garage is a room where a vehicle (a valued investment) can be appreciated, kept safe and dry, and stored or maintained until needed. Often the garage also serves as a workspace and storage space.
>
> Ideally, garages offer a comfortable and uplifting transition space that allows you to come and go from your home easily and auspiciously. It should be spacious, organized, well-lit, and uplifting.

Prime real estate

Although the tendency may be to think of the garage as a less important room, there is no such thing in Feng Shui! If the garage is attached to the home, it is a vital part of the homes energy imprint. Even if the garage is an outbuilding, it still has an energetic impact on the property and occupants of the property. It's important to also consider what is above and beside the garage. These spaces will most directly be affected by the energy of the garage, so creating a garage where vital Chi can flow in the garage will positively impact these spaces as well.

The items kept in your garage, and how they are being honored or not, have an impact on you and your space/life. Is your garage so overstuffed with toys, tools, equipment, and storage boxes that your car has to be parked outside? Is it so disorganized that things can't fit back in after being taken out? I see this all the time - prime real estate is filled with unloved and unorganized things (sometimes even future yard sale or donation items!) while expensive vehicles or pricey toys sit outside getting rained and snowed on!

Vehicles, toys, tools, and other things stored in the garage are an investment. Shouldn't these valuable and useful items be kept in a place of honor and care? Create a space that holds and respects these assets. Arrange it so that it's easy to access what you need and safely put it away when done.

What energy are you taking with you?

If you have a garage, it may be the room that you start and end your journey in each day. The energy created while you come and go is carried with you into the day ahead or back into your home. If your experience getting into and out of the car in the garage is easy, graceful and pleasant, your day will tend to follow that way. If your garage space is so jammed full of random stuff that it is hard to get in or out of the car, then coming and going becomes a frustrating chore each day. An unkempt garage is a less than ideal situation that poorly affects your energy every time you leave your house or come home after a busy day.

Consider the stuff that is in the garage and whether it is important enough to have that kind of powerful effect over your day/life. Take stock of the real value of the items stored in the garage verses the value of the automobiles, bikes, and tools that should be there. Consider the value of the mood it puts you in to deal with this situation daily. Is the stuff in the way really worth it?

Become aware of the simple energy that you encounter when you use this space to go in and out each day. What energy are you taking with you habitually? Would clearing out or better organizing some items in your garage make this transition more effortless and positive? Use that awareness to better prioritize the space so that it is empowering your day rather than depleting it. How do you want to feel when you come home every day, cramped and crabby or spacious and relaxed?

There are simple changes you can make to the garage to make it more positive. Even though it's not part of the living space, the garage can be arranged in a deliberately uplifting way. Spend some time considering what your real priorities are and what really deserves to be honored in this square footage. Purge whatever does not make the cut.

Organize items based on what they are used for and create separate areas as needed for each. Organize a potting bench in one area, tools for the home and car in a workshop corner. If you need to store items, create sturdy shelves and label what goes where. Make space on the floor or shelves for bikes and other toys so cleaning up and putting things away after use can be easy. Clear a space for the car with plenty of room around it to load in and out and work on the car if needed.

Finally, garages don't need to be dark and dirty. Even though it's "just a garage," it's often the first part of our home that we see when we come home. Upgrade the lighting to provide safety and ease when you're in the space. Add elements that will welcome you when you drive in each day, including but not limited to, freshly painted walls, a welcome sign, uplifting artwork, and even some decorative elements. This room should welcome you when you drive in. Add at least one item that makes you feel good/welcome as you come home.

One client asked me to consider the garage space with particular care. She ran a preschool out of her home. The children and their families were asked to enter through the garage because it was conveniently located near the coat storage and classroom. Although her garage was fairly neat and there was plenty of room for a pathway into the school, the client felt the garage entrance detracted from the playful learning experience she wanted the children to have as they arrived to start their school day. After considering the space and her needs, we came up with a plan to paint footprints on the garage floor that showed the children the way into the classroom space. In addition, she planned to paint a mural on the garage wall and the doorway between the garage and the classroom that reflected playful, kid-friendly scenes. A few cans of paint had the potential to shift the energy for everyone entering the school from warily entering a dark garage to skipping into a playful space. So fun!

Summary

Start looking at your garage as the important real estate that it is! Send yourself off with ease and welcome yourself home gracefully by shifting some energy in this space.

24 Other Household Systems

~ Nervous System ~ Respiratory System ~ Digestive System ~

Feng Shui isn't just about taking care of the furniture flow and décor, it's about taking care of the entire structure and all of the systems. The various systems in our house also have a subliminal meanings similar to the way the different structures, nooks, crannies, and passageways in home do. From plumbing to electrical wiring, to heating and ventilation systems, the condition and care of these systems can be an energetic reflection of what's going on in a home. Just like our bodies, our homes breathe, cleanse, and *experience emotions!* Often the condition of these household systems is a reflection of what's going on for the occupants.

Electrical wiring

The electrical wiring in our homes is a conduit, carrying information from one part of the house to another, turning things on and things off. It's similar to the nervous system in our own bodies, where chemical triggers send messages as impulses from one body system to the next. Power surges through the wires, outlets and breakers to power parts of our home just as synapses fire electrical or chemical impulses to power and direct our body parts and functions.

This energy flows through our homes unseen, but it affects the Chi flow of the space. In effect, electricity is chi. This charged, magnetized Chi surges through the house and interacts with the natural Chi of the land, the home, and our bodies. You may have heard the term EMF's, short for electro-magnetic frequencies. This energy is emitted from wiring, outlets, and appliances in our home. Many people consider it to be a detrimental form and flow of chi.

In general, how this energy is flowing and where it's being emitted around you can have an impact on your comfort and well-being. Electricity is a powerful conductor. You want to make sure that it is flowing in a safe, and beneficial way through out your home. When it flows in fits and starts, or leaks out of improperly wired systems, occupants of the house can feel the impact.

This energetic interference is unseen unless you use technology to measure it. But often analyzing the symptoms of what is going on in the house with the occupants, or in different life areas, can be a clue that something is not right with the electrical wiring. If you are sensitive enough you may be able to feel the fluctuations in the energy field caused by nearby appliances, faulty wiring and inefficient outlets when you walk into a room. For me, it can feel like the hair standing on the back of my neck or butterflies in my stomach. The space feels jittery.

For sure, the electrical system in the house is worth investigating further if someone in the home is having difficulty sleeping, is anxious or suffers from anxiety attacks, constantly feels drained (like a battery that's lost its charge), or frayed, like their "nerves are shot." Or maybe you've cleared clutter, moved stuff and Feng Shui'd everything but something still feels off. It's likely that the cause of the problem stems from a hidden household system.

Symptoms aside, it's still best to keep electrical appliances and devices to a minimum, especially in the bedroom. Turn off and unplug equipment that isn't in use. This simple act not only conserves energy but minimizes your exposure to potentially damaging energetic frequencies.

Plumbing systems

The pipes in our house carry purifying water into the home and move waste away from the home. In many ways the plumbing system mirrors the digestive system in the body.

Flowing water must go somewhere. If it can't move with ease it will build pressure until it breaks free, causing costly and often widespread damage. Even a small leak can ultimately create vast water damage to spaces. Ideally the water flows in easily and can drain out without obstructions.

In Feng Shui, flowing water represents flowing money. We certainly don't want any water leaking out anywhere in the system, as that is like money slowing draining away. And we want to avoid obstructions in the pipeline that energetically reflect the inability for things to keep flowing. Water is also related to emotions, particularly sadness or weepiness. If water is flowing freely, it's a sign that Chi is flowing freely too. There will be an ease and comfort in both emotional and financial wellbeing.

Certainly, if you're feeling financial pressure, and you've adjusted things without a positive result, it would be worthwhile checking to see if there is a plumbing blockage. If you feel like money is draining away from you, check for leaks in unseen areas and resolve them. Additionally, if occupants seem overly emotional and teary, and/or have consistent GI and digestive ailments, it could be a clue to check in on the health of the plumbing system.

Heating, air conditioning and ventilation systems

It's through these systems that a home breathes. When these are in good working order, fresh and temperate air can revitalize the space and support the occupants.

Keeping this equipment clean so that fresh air can enter and stagnant air can escape is critical to keeping the home and the occupants healthy. Systems that exchange air or move it from one space to another can play a significant role in spreading germs too. Clean systems equal clean air, which equals healthy and vital occupants in the space. In the event of consistent illness, especially, respiratory health issues, the HVAC system should be checked.

Placement of the vents, exhaust and drainage lines from an HVAC system can have a big impact on the quality and comfort in a space. For safety and health reasons, make sure exhaust pipes are clear of any obstruction, and that inside vents direct air in a supportive way. Having hot or cold air blowing directly on you while you work or sleep is often unpleasant and can have health consequences. Keep all of the equipment maintained regularly so that it is in working order even during extremes of temperature. No one is content when the air conditioner breaks on a hot day or a heating unit shuts down in the dead of winter.

Summary

All of the household systems have an impact on the wellbeing of the residents. Additionally, these systems have a big effect on the natural Chi flow in a space. They were invented long after the practice of Feng Shui began, and they are known for artificially changing and moving the Chi in a space. The changes to the natural energy flow that these systems create, as well as the subtle, hidden energies given off by their fixtures has a tremendous potential to affect the wellbeing of occupants. Knowing where you sit and sleep, in relation to where the major elements of these systems are, is vital. Keeping them in good working order is critical to the health of the house and of the people who live there.

25 Landscapes

~ Directing and Holding Chi ~

~ Harmoniously Connecting Inside and Outside ~

> Your home or business should be easy to find, and easy to get to, with plenty of parking Ideally it would be surrounded by other thriving homes and businesses.
>
> Signs of fresh vibrant Chi around a building include other vibrant structures, lots of greenery, natural elements, and landscaping and hardscaping that emphasize a protected and vital space.

What's going on around you

Applying Feng Shui inside of a house or building is not all there is. It's also incredibly powerful to take a step outside of the space you occupy and see what's going on out there. Is the energy flow outside able to get in to nourish you? Is the outside space in order and kept well, so that good energy is coming your way? What kind of energy is being directed at you from other neighbors, other structures or even natural objects in the outside area?

Go stand on your front steps and look around to see what catches your attention. Is there anything pointing at your front door that would send energy in a jarring way towards your space? Look for large trees, power lines, electrical boxes, sharp angles on nearby buildings. Perhaps the way your neighbor's house is angled sends a stream of sharp and cutting energy toward your front door. It's important to be aware of this so that you can make corrections to ease and balance the type and flow of the energy that's coming to your front door. Look around your home and property for any energies that can be adjusted for.

© Laurie Mounce

Consider how your street directs energy to or away from you: If your home is positioned on a straight roadway, you may find that natural Chi is pulled right past you. If you live on a cul-de-sac, the Chi tends to gather and collide because of the circular dead end nature of the road. Ideally, the street is wide and gently curves back and forth with houses equally set on both sides. When the street is not ideal you'll need to do some work to call the Chi toward your house.

Take a walk or a drive around your surrounding block or neighborhood and get a sense and feel for the energy of the area. Notice places with stagnant energy such as a neighbor's house that is unattended, or an empty field where construction was halted.These can all be directing less than positive energy toward your space. Signs of positive Chi surrounding your home/business include other thriving homes and businesses, a park full of laughing children, lots of greenery and flowers.

© Kerri Miller

In the landscape, Feng Shui adjustments can be made to balance and regulate the Chi flow as it comes to the property. Colorful paint, good lighting, or a welcome flag could all help draw energy from the road towards the house. Negative influences like unpleasant views, traffic flow, or an electrical box can be neutralized by placing outdoor furniture or plantings to strategically to redirect or block the flow.

Enhancements can be placed in the yard, like bird feeders, fountains, or garden ornaments to adjust for the shape of the landscaping, block something unpleasant, or call good Chi towards the home.

An ideal Feng Shui landscape for a home has a protective cradle around the home (tall trees or a ridge or hill behind the home is ideal for protection. In front of the home the view ought to be flat and sweeping, so you can see what is approaching. In this way the home is in the command position and Chi flows toward it and is gently held around it. If your property does not offer this naturally, you can use landscaping to help direct and hold the Chi in a positive way. Good outside Chi will help support and provide better Chi flow to the inside of the house too.

Consider the whole house

Hopefully now you have an informed view of how your home and the stuff you keep can contribute to supporting your personal energy or depleting it. If you take anything away from this book I hope it's that homes are not just structures, they are physical bodies of energy that work in similar ways to our own body. They have a heart, they have memory, and they breathe and thrive. And, just like our human bodies they can be nourished or depleted, healthy or unwell.

We've explored the natural energy flow called chi.

We've explored how the arrangement of our space and the items we choose to put there affect that energy flow and that of the occupants.

We've looked at the hidden meaning of each part of the home and the ideal ways to arrange each room for positive energy flow.

Now, in the next section, lets pull it all together into a process you can follow to apply in your space to evoke positive change in all areas of you home and life. You'll be able to create a space that feels better and flows better.

SECTION FOUR

Feng Shui for Inspired Living

Step by Step

Section 4 – Introduction

In the previous sections I've given you the tip of the iceberg regarding Feng Shui principles and how energy flows. Is there more to learn? You bet! After more than a decade of study I'm still learning about this amazing stuff every day. But with this general understanding of the topic and a desire to pay attention to the energy that surrounds us all I've made dramatic shifts in my own life and helped others make big shifts too.

Some believe that only masters of Feng Shui study should be consulted in these matters and these tools shouldn't be available for just anyone to tinker with. On the contrary, I believe most of this knowledge is innate to all of us and we just need a reminder to pay attention and consider it. I truly believe everyone can benefit from working with this wisdom on their own and that's why I'm summarizing the very basics here for all to use.

Of course there are occasions when consulting a Feng Shui Professional instead of doing it yourself is recommended. I'll talk about some of these situations in Chapter 28. I trust that you'll know when you'll need to reach out for support and guidance, and in the meantime I think you can play with what you know and use it to create a more dynamic and intentioned future for yourself.

In the next section I'll show you step by step how to take what we've been talking about all along and put it into practice in your own home to support the life that you want. Feng Shui is a seriously effective medium but can be very fun and empowering too. Read through the next section: soak it in, practice it, move stuff around, and then move it back. Mostly just enjoy it and don't be too serious. I assure you'll get better results that way.

26 Create a Space That Feels Better and Flows Better

You can do this! It's time to take a look at how to apply this new understanding of energy, your spaces and your stuff to your own personal space so that it feels better, flows better and supports all of your life aspirations. This section will explain where to start making changes and what practice to follow each time you are looking to freshen your space or change it to support a particular life area, life change or goal. This is the method I've used with clients for more than a decade now, and with the understanding you've gained in this book you can benefit from it on your own.

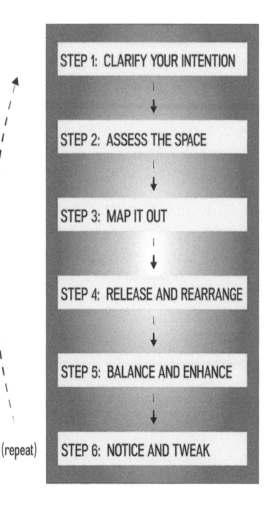

STEP 1: CLARIFY YOUR INTENTION

STEP 2: ASSESS THE SPACE

STEP 3: MAP IT OUT

STEP 4: RELEASE AND REARRANGE

STEP 5: BALANCE AND ENHANCE

(repeat)

STEP 6: NOTICE AND TWEAK

Step 1: Clarify your intention

By now you know that Feng Shui is not just about moving furniture around, and you've probably realized that it's more than clearing clutter from your space. Feng Shui provides an opportunity to take an in depth look at each area of your life, and make adjustments that encourage support, ease, and harmony for your whole self. The real benefit to using Feng Shui comes when you first clarify what it is that you want to deliberately create or support with your Feng Shui changes. Then, when you begin moving things around in your space, you can do it with a clear intention and a purpose that will have a significant effect.

Begin by considering your current life situations and how you intend them to be better. Consider each of your personal nine Life Areas and note what is working for you in each area. Do you feel completely fulfilled in each area, including having a career (life journey) that inspires you, a relationship that completes you, and so on for each of nine categories? Do you want more creative time, stronger relationships with your family members, or more financial security? When it's recognized that a life area is not as fulfilling as desired, then it becomes clear where you should begin your work.

Once you've chosen a Life Area to work with, notice what's working, and what isn't in that area. Considering this will bring clarity about what's missing, what could improve, and ultimately what goals you want to pursue and support in this piece of your life. Notice, preferably without judgement or emotion, where the disconnect is between where you are and where you want to be. Rather than focusing on what is wrong or missing, or getting caught up in not knowing how to get from where you are to where you want to be, just simply consider what it is that you want to be different. Some people find it helpful to then create a list of what they want to shift in each life area.

Less is More

You may find that you'd like to see changes in a few different life areas, but I encourage you to pick one and work on it solely. You can address the others at a later time. If you were to work on multiple areas at once, and make significant changes all around, it's hard to know which changes worked and which ones didn't. Sometimes you may need to tweak or undo some changes you've made if you have unexpected results. If you've addressed too much at once you'll be challenged in the event you have to backtrack. Approaching the whole process with a slow and steady mentality will bring you the most success.

EXAMPLE: Let's take the example of Kate. Kate is a single professional woman who owns a small two story colonial house. She's been frustrated with her job for a while now and she's considering a career change. She knows she wants to put some deliberate thought into the Fulfilling Work area of her life. She starts by making a list of the things she doesn't like about her current position in Sales: it's a long commute, the job is stressful and she has little support, there's no growth potential and overall the line of work is not very fulfilling or inspiring. From that list it's easy to see what she wants is a more fulfilling job with growth potential and a short commute! After a little more soul searching, she admits that she's always wanted to be a teacher. Maybe she could apply for a transfer to her company's training department, where she could facilitate the training workshops. Kate also wants to be in a relationship again, so she's considering whether to work on the Relationship area of her life instead. She was in a long term partnership that ended a few years ago. Since then she's been on a few dates but nothing seems worth pursuing. She knows she wants to find her soul mate: someone around her age, who enjoys similar interests like hiking and travel and who would share her love of dogs. She wants to be with someone that's ready to take the next step and start a family at some point. Kate decides its best to get her own life in order first, before pursuing a relationship, so she decides to focus on the career changes. Now she has more clarity about her situations, and she can decide what the next step is. Things are already looking up!

Step 2: Assess the space

Take some time to walk through to generally assess your home. Do this when it's at its most real state, the way it would be after a day of living and being in the space. I always ask my clients not to clean or put things away before I come to visit, because I want to see the true flow of energy. This is best assessed by seeing where things like clutter congest or where areas are sparse and rigid.

As you walk through, notice what is jumping out at you and what message it might have for you. If you look at a cluttered bookshelf and cringe, realize (without judging and without taking any action) that this is energetically what you're up against every day, usually without paying attention to it. It's important to notice it without trying to fix it. The more you sit with it, the more messages and possible solutions will come to light.

Continue walking through and make note of things that you love and things that are bothering you. Notice if you have to move around anything uncomfortable (the Chi will also be struggling around it), and pay attention to where things have landed during your typical day. Take note of how your body feels, lightness, heaviness, ease, unease, and any emotions that come up for you, anxiety, happiness, unworthiness, calmness. These reactions are always there, but now you're taking the time to notice and acknowledge them. Those subliminal messages you're getting from the things in your space are eye-opening! If you're like I was before I discovered Feng Shui, you've probably never taken the time to consider your space this way before. Take a moment to jot down some notes about your new observations.

A picture is worth a thousand words

I'll talk about this in more detail shortly, but for now know that it's helpful to take photos of each of the rooms in your house and look at them carefully in addition to walking through your space and feeling how it feels. Photos often show us things we avoid noticing with our eyes. They can often reveal secrets we might not see otherwise. Give it a try!

EXAMPLE: Kate takes a walk through her house. There are a few things that stand out to her because they make her feel really good, a picture of the dog she rescued, some handmade dishware she bought on a trip a few years back, and the bedroom set that once belonged to her grandmother. Other things she looks at feel heavier, like the bookshelf that is "simply a mess," and the desk that was picked out by her old boyfriend (which she immediately realizes she never liked anyway!) She feels overwhelmed as she finally takes a close look at the damage that has occurred from a leaky toilet (she's been ignoring that for months) and acknowledges piles of clutter in several rooms. Kate realizes that her home is currently a pretty clear reflection of her mind-set lately. Because she's been so stressed at work she hasn't been taking care of things around the house or putting much attention into making it feel inviting. What happened? She used to love her house and it used to make her feel really happy to come home to it. Now it just feels "eh." She's a bit disheartened, but realizes she's ready for change. Kate jots down a list of what she discovered and some ideas for how she wants it to be.

Step 3: Map it out

Here is where I think the real fun and opportunity comes in with Feng Shui. You've lined up some energy behind what you want, but the universe provides so much more energy to support you. Imagine if on top of simply clarifying, assessing, and adjusting things, you could draw upon the ancient knowledge of chi's power in your space to support what it is you're after next?

Now you can use the Bagua Map to support the specific Life Area that you want to bring change to. You'll be able to take what you've learned about yourself and the space you keep and apply some Feng Shui techniques to create even more powerful change toward the life you want. You'll learn more about yourself and your space, and you'll be able to harness what you need to direct positive changes in any part of your life.

Begin by drawing out your floorplan and applying the Bagua Map over it as described in Chapter 5. Draw a bird's eye view of your home as accurately and to scale as possible for the best result, but don't get too caught up in the details. Make sure to note the entrances to each room, windows and location of major pieces of furniture. Draw the Bagua Map over your house rendering and note the location of each of the life area Guas. Now you can consider your space again and see where different sections of your house correspond to each Life Area.

As you review your space in relation to the Bagua Map, you might notice that Life Areas you have found challenging correlate to challenging spaces in your home, to areas that collect clutter easily, or to areas you have identified that haven't been working well for you. It's common to see challenging Life Areas align with parts of the home that have natural challenges, like a bathroom, an unusable space, or a space that symptomatically collects clutter or feels unstable.

Now take a look at the map and identify what part of the house falls into the life area you've decided to work on. Go to that area in your house and repeat step two just in this area while considering its relationship to the challenges you have. Notice what room it is, consider how the room works or not, look for signs of clutter and arrangements that would cause negative chi. Identify things in the space that might be creating a pattern that is unsupportive of your newly clarified goals for that Life Area. Now you can focus more intently on this area of your house that is related to the Gua you want to shift and make changes that are positive and supportive.

Maybe as you do this process, you notice that the Life Area you want to work on falls outside of your home – the area is missing. Consider if that newly found information correlates to how things are going for you at work. Just notice! Don't panic! It's not ideal but you can now take this information and make changes that will directly benefit your goals for this area of your life. In addition to remedying the missing area by using landscaping to anchor the missing part of the home, you can also enhance this particular life area in each individual room. (Note: Chapter 5 contains more tips on what to do if the area you want to work on is "missing".)

EXAMPLE: Kate draws out the layout of her house and consults her trusty Feng Shui book to reference the Bagua Map. After laying the map over her drawing she sees that her front doorway and entryway fall in the Fulfilling Work area of the house. Above the entryway on the second floor, it is a bathroom that falls into that Gua also. She goes to both of these areas to investigate further. The front entryway is her least favorite part of the house. It's always a mess and particularly so lately. The "welcome table" is piled high with some bags from her last business trip. And since she didn't take time to store it away last spring, her winter gear is hanging behind the door, making it so crowded that she can't even open it all the way. The one piece of artwork in the space is a crooked picture she had randomly picked up at the craft store. Just standing there makes her feel that usual rushed feeling she feels every morning as she frantically tries to find what she needs to get out to work on time. Ugh! Kate notes the leaky upstairs bathroom toilet again. She notes how she spends a fair amount of time in this room each day getting ready. Perhaps if this room had a bit more style she might feel a bit more jazzed about starting her day. Well no wonder she feels stressed and uninspired at work – the spaces related to Fulfilling Work are stressful and uninspiring too!

Apply the Bagua in layers

Want to support a particular Life Area even further? You don't have to stop after working with the space in your home that corresponds with the life area on the Bagua Map. You can add more layers of positive energy by taking some time to declutter, organize and enhance other related spaces: the table you work from at home, a home office if you have one, and of course your actual desk, cubicle, or office at your work place. Simply taking the time to clarify what you want is amazing! Then, enhancing the career area in each room of your home and your work workspaces will have amazing results!

Step 4: Release and rearrange

You've identified the shifts that you'd like to make in your life. You've reconnected with the spaces in the home and the things you keep in it and recognized what needs to shift physically in your space. You've correlated your space with the Bagua Map to see how it relates back to the life areas. Now it's time to look at your space with the new view and re-think how you can deliberately set up each space to support yourself and all the occupants.

First, release the things you've identified in your space that have less than ideal energy. Remember that clutter is anything that is no longer supporting you positively. Clutter can weigh you down, cause overwhelm, and prevent nourishing energy from getting to you. Releasing anything that's not useful, loved or well honored will open up space for Chi to flow and allow new opportunities to come to light. You may find that as you begin to release unneeded stuff you get even more clarity about what you want to create. Maybe you even start to get some intuitive hits or previously unseen resolutions suddenly start to become clear. This is a sure sign that the Chi is starting to flow in the right direction!

This is especially important in the part of the house related to the Life Area you want to make changes in. Clear out the clutter, give the space a good cleaning, let go of unsupportive items and any artwork or symbols that aren't serving your goal. Ideally you are left with items you love and that are useful, supportive and inspiring!

Next, rearrange whatever is left so that it's pleasing to see and easy to gracefully move in and around. With your intentions for the space and the related Life Area in mind, deliberately arrange the items that are left. Take a look at the tips given for the room in question in Section #3 to make sure the space set up in the most nourishing way. Place furniture in the command position where called for, move obstacles out of the way, and make sure all the necessities are there and organized usefully.

Consider Chi flow as you go. The goal here is to place whatever you've chosen to keep in a way that allows the energy to move freely throughout the space. Sometimes only simple adjustments are necessary to help it flow more supportively. If you can pass easily through the space without hesitation or having to dodge around things you are on track. Test the area out by using it and seeing how it flows. Try out each seat or work as needed in the space to see how you feel as you are there. Make corrections as needed. Once you've rearranged the area in a way that feels better and flows better it should quickly begin to feel much more positive!

By eliminating the clutter, you've removed an obstacle to Chi flow to the area of your life that needs improvement. Things that don't support you have been removed and other things left are now arranged in a way that feels better and flows better. The space will be feeling much more positive already, but there's still a chance to add a few extra touches that really energize the space and enhance your intentions for this part of your life. In the next step you can mindfully consider how to support your goals within your space even further.

EXAMPLE: Kate knows exactly what needs to be done in both areas now. She starts outside, by sweeping off her front walkway and steps. She can't remember the last time she did that! Inside she packs away out-of-season clothes and shoes and finally puts away the bags from her trip. She moves the entry table so it's better placed to hold keys and mail. The door can now finally open all the way and it's much easier to find what she needs and get in and out. Upstairs she goes through bathroom cabinets and drawers clearing out anything she no longer uses. She makes arrangements for the toilet to be repaired and gives the whole space a good cleaning. Both areas look and feel better already, and she's noticing that getting to work is less harried. Even her days at her dead end job feel better and less stressed!

Step 5: Balance and enhance

I consider this step the icing on the cake. It's where you can really charge up your space with intentioned Chi enhancements that harness and direct the energy in the space to jumpstart the changes you want to see.

First, take a look at how the elements are represented in your space. Can all five elements – water, earth, metal, fire and wood – be found in the space? If any of the elements are over or under represented, make some corrections by adding or removing things to create better balance. Using the natural cycles of the elements as discussed in Chapter 4 is powerful here if you want to play with it.

In general, having all five elements in view will energetically create harmony and balance in the room which can reflect on the related Life Area. Try it! It's a very subtle but soothing change.

Highlighting the five elements in your décor

Make subliminal changes to your space by simply rearranging what's in the room so there are groupings that contain all five elements placed in a few prominent areas around the room. This can be as simple as adding a fish tank which naturally has all five elements, or creating an arrangement of a few decorative items that each represent an element on a table or a shelf. It's a simple way to settle any space.

Next, consider what you can bring into your space to make it more appealing, and simultaneously support the kind of energy you want to create and the goals you wish to manifest.

Are there colors, artwork, and other symbols that would better represent what you want from your career? Bring them in and place them with the clear intention that you want to energize this part of your life.

Consider whether you need to add any additional cures or enhancements to the space such as a crystal to further lift and circulate the Chi in this area, a mirror to reflect and double the energy of what you want to create, or a plant to encourage healthy growth. There are many possibilities here that will help bring energy and awareness to the space and related life area.

Caution

As you're adding things to balance the elements, symbolize your goals or further activate Chi in the space be sure that you're not adding more stuff that ultimately isn't serving you. Make sure everything you add is something you love and that energizes you!

It's quite amazing what can happen once you clarify what you want/ need and deliberately set up your space with that in mind. Once you set your mind to where change would be beneficial, energy literally starts moving and life starts shifting. It still amazes me. That's why I love Feng Shui so much. Generally, you'll see positive results in a very short period of time by just putting a bit of extra attention to these steps.

EXAMPLE: Although both spaces related to Kate's Fulfilling Work area are much improved, she wants to add some specific enhancements that will further help support her aspirations for that part of her life. She replaces the old picture in the entry with an inspiring piece that reads "YOU CAN DO THIS!" She finds a small lamp to put on her welcome table. To add extra "oomph" to her job transfer request she's printed out the job description and hidden it under the lamp, and she keeps the light turned on a few extra hours each day. Upstairs in the bathroom she's started regularly using her "fancy" towels that used to just be reserved for guests. She also added two large healthy plants to represent the growth she would like to see in her career.

6. Notice and tweak

You're now surrounded in this space with things that have been deliberately placed to support your newfound clarity. You may be ready to dive into changing another area of your house that is related to another challenging life area. Stop! Wait.

Sit with the changes that you've made for a few days and notice how it all feels. Remember that you're not just moving things around here. You're shifting energy. The effects of shifts you make are often invisible but rippling. If you change too much at once you can create overwhelm when everything feels different at once. In the event something feels off, you want to be able to backtrack easily and adjust things as needed.

Ideally the space will feel better and everyone within will seem to be thriving a little better. Pay attention to any shifts or changes happening in your life. Are your days moving along with ease and grace (hopefully even more than before the changes) or are you hitting a few unexpected bumps in the road. Do you feel better when you come into the space? Does the area seem to flow better since making adjustments? Are relationships faring well since the changes? Follow your intuition and tweak things as needed for a few days or even weeks. You should see some consistent benefit before moving forward to address another Life Area.

EXAMPLE: Kate is pretty proud of all the work she's done. It wasn't easy but she is happy with the results. Even though she's applied for a job transfer and is hoping it comes through soon, these simple changes have already helped her feel more content, confident and able to handle all the things her current job is sending her way! She can't wait to start making some Feng Shui changes next weekend, to support another goal—making room for the perfect partner!

Summary

I hope you can see now how playing with Feng Shui can have a positive impact on any life situation. Deliberately choosing what you keep and how you keep will help support you in both subliminal and obvious ways. Some of it may even seem like common sense! But when you pay attention to it all you can approach life in a very supported and empowered way.

27 Adding A Sacred Element to Your Space

On top of deliberately arranging your space with your aspirations and Feng Shui in mind, you can also take steps to make your space more revered and sacred. It's these mindful extra touches that can energetically charge the space with positive vibes. These "frosting on the cake" extra touches will truly add energy to your space. In essence it will love you back, helping you and all the occupants to thrive.

What is it that makes a space feel extra special? In my opinion, a space has that quality when extra special touches have been added. To treat something sacredly is to care for it, embellish it, and honor it. What extra special touches can you do in your home that will give it that extra sparkle and buzz? Here are a few ideas:

1. **Give it a name.** Whether it's your home, a room you're in all the time, or your car, take time to honor the space by giving it a name. Not only does this create a stronger connection between you and your space but it also signifies pride, respect and ownership of it. This relationship with your space encourages further care and keeping. You become more vested in caring for and keeping the space. It's a symbolic honor to bestow on a place you frequent. An extra special touch.

2. **Keep the energy clean.** Regularly clear the space energetically and take the time to set intentions and bless the space. It's particularly powerful to do a space clearing and blessing before having company. Set intentions for the event and create an energetically clear space for it to take place. After guests have gone, take time clear the space again.

3. **Arrange an altar.** Create a sacred area of your home where you can place symbols of what you seek and offerings of gratitude. Make this a space that you attend to often, changing things out, refining intentions, meditating and visualizing. Create a space where you can connect to your higher self and receive intuitive guidance and support.

4. **Burn a candle, burn incense, or diffuse essential oils into the space.** These are sacred practices that have been used for centuries to add energy to a space and to clear negative vibrations. When you don't have time to do a full space clearing, at least light a candle or incense. Taking the extra time to add in this cleansing and uplifting ritual to parts of your home and parts of your day helps slow you down, reminds you to be aware, and connects you to unseen energies.

5. **Turn off the gadgets for a regular period of time.** We get used to hearing TV as background noise. It becomes comfortable. Turn it off and spend some time listening to the sounds of your space, the songs of nature outside, and perhaps you will even hear snippets of your own higher knowledge. Trust me when I tell you that your home and surroundings do talk to you and will give you guidance; you just have to allow quiet and sacred time into your day in order

to be able to hear it.

6. **Slow down and take the time to make everything a bit extra special.** Set the table with your favorite dishes, light candles, create a fabulous meal with fresh ingredients, make the bed. Instead of moving through our day unconsciously, taking the time to add these extra special touches will break you out of mindless habits, slow you down and connect you to your actions and your space more deliberately. It will shift the vibe of your actions and your space.

Life is a miracle, nature is full of magic, and your home is a sacred space where you can connect to this higher realm of energy and vitality, especially if you slow down, put rituals and ceremonies in place, and create the waiting atmosphere to connect with it.

28 Practical Tips

Through the years of working with others to help them better align their spaces, I've learned a few tricks that help people get started and keep moving forward through the process even when the going gets tough. If you've got a room that seems impossible to tackle or that you have no idea where to start, or if you've started the process and then stumbled, some of these ideas may help you.

Keep your eyes on the prize.

Don't just consider the project that's sitting in front of you, but look ahead to how it will look and feel when it's done. Even more, consider how having been through the process will open up clarity and opportunity for you. Be open to the possibility ahead instead of just the challenge in front.

When you need a jumpstart

If you have a space you want to work on but just can seem to get started, it can be a result of the stuck energy that's present.

- **Get the energy moving enough to encourage you to dive in.** Some ways include opening the windows and doors, turning on the lights in the room and leaving them on for a while, putting a fan on in the room, or hanging a faceted crystal from the ceiling in the center of the room. These will help begin to circulate the energy and you'll soon feel compelled to get to work.

- **Sit there for twenty minutes**. I've often recommended making time to just go into the challenging room and just sit and look around. Notice what's bothering you, consider the options you have, and just be with all the input you're getting while in the space. I guarantee you won't be able to stand it for long. Suddenly you'll start noticing that something needs to move, you'll recognize things you no longer need, and a plan will start coming together. You'll be taking action in no time!

- **Set a timer and accomplish a little at a time**. Finally, I've always found it helpful to give yourself about fifteen minutes a day to do something in the room. One night you open a box and see what's inside. The next night you sort it onto the floor. The next night you purge some of it. The next night you organize what's left. In two to three weeks you'll have made a big dent in the space. More often than not, when I start working on it this way, I end up staying longer and getting far more done, faster than expected.

The challenge often is just getting started. Once you're past that point momentum will be on your side.

Try focusing elsewhere

It's tempting to dive right in and work on your most chronically challenged area first. Whether you've been dealing with extended health issues, financial hardship or can't find the right partner, the desire to find a solution once and for all will send you to work tirelessly on that area. Often though, it's best to look away from that struggle for a time and focus on another less challenged life area first. Sometimes there's just too much confused energy around the situation already, so working at it from every angle just complicates it. Try one of these tactics instead:

Start with a life area you have less energy vested in. Often, focusing elsewhere still leads to resolution by a simple domino effect; once one area is loosened up the rest falls into place more easily.

- **Look at the opposite Gua.** When one area is challenging, it also helps to look at the Gua that is directly opposite of it and work on that location/life area. These opposite Guas are related and play off of one another, so shifting one can support changes in the other. For example, a Fulfilling work life is very much related to the Recognition that is received in life and work; Partnerships are stronger when each individual has a strong connection to their own Guidance; the ability to receive Abundance is connected to how much Support you have. These life areas are connected and work off of each other in a very dynamic way that can be used to help shift things beneficially.

- **Only work on one area at a time**. I mentioned this in the last chapter but it's worth repeating. Remember that you're not just moving things around and purging things. You're also shifting unseen energies that can have a significant effect on the space and the occupants. This somewhat depends on your situation and your personal energetic constitution, but I have found that sometimes, when too many changes are undertaken at once it can feel chaotic and unsettling at first. This makes is it hard to hold the energy of the changes that have been made. Sometimes, too much, too fast, can set you back instead of move you forward. In addition, if you make several changes at once, it can be hard to tell which ones worked and which ones presented challenges. It's much better to shift something and then sit with it for a while, becoming aware of the new energy and getting used to it before making another significant change. Sometimes Less is More!

A picture *IS* worth a thousand words

Pictures are a wonderful tool to use when implementing Feng Shui in your space. They have the ability to capture things that are just not clear to the naked eye. You can be in a room looking around for hours and then look at a picture of the same space taken at the same time, and you will notice new things or see things in a way that you hadn't when you were in the space.

Pictures allow a bit of a filter between what's going on in the room and the sensation of it all. I find that referencing an image allows me to notice what's going on in a room without getting all emotional about it. They are truly priceless tools in this way.

Take pictures of the space BEFORE you start making changes. I always encourage people to do this. There are several reasons for this.

> **First**, you may get into the middle of the project and freak out. The mess will be bigger than ever and you'll get discouraged, feeling like you've been working harder than ever and accomplishing little positive result. Looking at the before pictures and remembering what wasn't working then will help you move forward.

> **Second**, when you get done and are able to look back on how far you have come you'll be encouraged the next time you want to jump into making changes.

> **Third**, sometimes you'll see solutions by looking at the picture that you wouldn't otherwise notice.

> **Finally**, it's always fun to have bragging rights after working on a big project! I kick myself whenever I

dive into making changes without snapping a picture first!

Commit to go easy on yourself

No matter what state you and your house are in when you start this process, cut yourself some slack. Nobody is perfect, and you've probably navigated life pretty well so far without having much knowledge of how all this unseen energy is affecting you. Now that you are aware you may be troubled by the challenges you face and the way you've been keeping your stuff until now. It can be very easy to waste a whole lot of time kicking yourself, judging your situation and being your own worst critic. I can assure you that is not going to get you to a better place. It will stop you from moving forward and it is really just a reflex to keep you stuck. Instead, pat yourself on the back for surviving this far, step into your place of power and start working with what you've learned in this book. It won't take much before you're seeing and feeling things shift in a more positive way.

Keep in mind that applying Feng Shui is not an overnight process where you flip a switch and things shift for the better. It takes some practice, and some trial and error. Give yourself the space and time to implement it. You'll never be done with the process either! We are ever evolving in new directions and setting new goals for ourselves. Feng Shui is something that ideally shifts in stages to support that growth.

Use the buddy system

Ask a friend to come by for a few hours and help you decide what is useful to keep and what you should let go of. Someone who is separated from the emotions of the stuff will be able to keep you on track. A second set of eyes is always helpful for deciding what clothes to keep in your closet, which pictures should be hung where, and which color works best on that wall. In my Feng Shui Practice I offer optional coaching services along with my consultations. When you are by yourself you can get stuck on the little things. You can clear a bookshelf but then get stuck on figuring out where to move the discarded books. You can get into the middle of your closet and get discouraged because the clothes don't fit as well as you'd like. A partner helps walk you through these emotional snags so that you can keep moving forward on your project. Of course make sure to choose a buddy who will not judge the situation and jump into the drama and emotion with you, but will be able to keep you on track.

Evaluate often

As we live and grow and have new experiences we evolve and change. Our circumstances, likes and dislikes shift all the time. Last summer I was spending some time with my family and working as a Practitioner; fast forward six months and I'm now deep in the process of writing and creating. My goals have changed, and I have different needs and desires as a result. I'm in my office now more than ever. It's cleaner than ever too because I need to keep a clean slate for this creative process. The rest of my house, on the other hand … well let's just say the dust bunnies are bigger than ever! Situations change and needs change, often rapidly. Because of that I encourage everyone to check in with their spaces and evaluate their current needs on a regular basis. If you address it regularly in small bites it will not become a big overwhelming project that's hard to take on.

Maybe you could check in once a year at the New Year. Perhaps every six months works for you. I tend to do it at the change of seasons – at least three to four times a year. Maybe you cycle through and check off a room a month. Figure out what works best for you. Often when I'm changing out seasonal clothes it's the perfect time to purge what no longer fits. You can look at other possessions and areas of the home in the same way. At a minimum, consider a spring clean-up and a fall refresher. You will feel the energy shift every time you put some energy into your space.

Perhaps there are no changes to make at all, but at least you've done the check in. The point is to be connected to your space so that you "hear" when it's time to make a change -- just like I did when I was a little girl and was subliminally feeling the itch to shift things. The point is to pay attention and notice when things are feeling off so that you can adjust as needed.

This doesn't mean you completely redo every space over and over. It just means simply check in. Maybe that picture isn't something you love anymore. Maybe you're not in a relationship now and want to create more space to include another. Perhaps the kids have grown and are out of the house now and it's time to reclaim some space for you. The important thing is to check in regularly, make a few changes that reflect how you've grown or changed – or perhaps you make changes based on a new goal or desire you'd like to manifest. Be aware of your needs and keep your space in line with what you need. Over time you'll be happy that you stayed on top of it by evaluating often.

Doing it yourself verses hiring a Feng Shui professional

As I mentioned in the introduction to this section, I'm a proponent of the do-it-yourself method of applying Feng Shui. Many of my offerings as a Feng Shui consultant are geared toward empowering people to be able to communicate with their own space. I want to give you the tools you need to create huge shifts in your life. I strongly believe that each of you has your own innate ability to know what you need, and apply important cures, with little support.

That said, there are those times that are overwhelming when support is called for. With all personal challenges and growth opportunities, it's often difficult to see past the challenges and find the solutions alone. Sometimes the problem is too blinding and old habits and patterns are too tangled: you can feel it's impossible to break free and create new pathways without support from another.

A fresh set of eyes on the subject is always beneficial. Call on someone to help you when needed. They'll be able to look at the situation from a different perspective and a place of clarity that you simply don't have when immersed in the situation. Two sets of eyes are better than one!

In addition, I can assure you that a Feng Shui Professional has more customized cures, tricks and tools up their sleeve than you could ever find in a book, article, or online program. The shifts and changes that I recommend are individually inspired by the clients' reflections, what I see in the space, and lots of experience and intuitive support. I get great results when working with clients because of these proficiencies and instincts. If you practice on your own, you will see changes, but they just might be smaller and slower to take effect than if you were working on it with a specialist.

If a problem is chronic, and you keep finding yourself in the midst of the same unsupportive pattern, it's probably time to drop the do-it-yourself method and call in the troops for support. Consider the cost of continuing to keep on struggling by yourself. If you are risking financial ruin, a lost relationship, or years stuck in a dead-end job, it may be time to invest in a solution. Consider the cost of hiring a consultant and/or coach to guide you through identifying the changes that need to be made and to support you through the process. It is probably far less than the emotional, financial, and time consuming costs associated with ignoring the problems and avoiding the potential solutions.

Working with this stuff yourself first is encouraged. Empower yourself with these tools to create change in your life, but be open to seeking professional help with it if you don't see the patterns changing. Feng Shui is about much more than making your space feel better. It's about shifting energy permanently to support all of your life areas and harnessing energy to create a life you love!

29 Summary

This is the end of the book but the beginning of your Feng Shui journey. I began my Feng Shui journey by reading one simple book about Feng Shui and then beginning to apply what I learned in my space and my life. I believe it has been tremendously empowering tool to use through the years to deliberately guide my life in the direction that I wanted it to go. I wish for this to be the beginning for you as well, providing you with a tool that can support the life you want to live. Whether this introduction leads you to the next book, to practicing on your own space, or to calling in professional Feng Shui support, consider yourself armed with a new understanding of how to direct energies to your best benefit.

I think it's important to note that there is a cost of not acknowledging energy flow and how it affects you and your space. There's a cost to simply surviving. Many people settle for where they are for various reasons, but at great loss. It's amazing to me how many people I run into who are awed to hear about Feng Shui and its benefits and who exclaim they could greatly benefit from the changes, and then they continue on their current path. People are afraid of change on so many levels. Perhaps they worry things can get worse, they fear the effort they'll need to put in, or perhaps they are simply put off by the fear of the unknown.

It's all well and good to keep pressing on, until you consider the cost for putting up with all that is. What are you missing out on? How could things be better for you? What would it feel like to be thriving instead of simply getting by? Maybe you have Oprah potential! What if the cure for cancer is just an energetic shift away for you? What if your true mate is on the other side of that Feng Shui shift?

There is proven potential to this amazing tool called Feng Shui, but first you must admit that there is more real potential in your own life. Why wait until you get SO uncomfortable that you have no other choice but to consider Feng Shui as a tool. Don't wait until your marriage is at the breaking point, your business is not thriving, your health is in decline? Feng Shui can help you avert or skirt around those kinds of challenges with much more ease! It's a new empowering tool. Take it and run with it. Enjoy the journey!

Section Four Credits

Six step process copyrighted by Marty McCagg

More Feng Shui Resources

Are you intrigued by what you've learned about feng shui so far? Want more?? There are many options available for those who are looking for more support with Feng Shui!

Private Consultations for Residences and Businesses – Kerri is available for consultations onsite or via video call. Multiple levels of support are available depending upon your specific needs. She can also provide assistance in finding a consultant near you.

Clutter Clearing Support – Kerri is available to support you through your clutter clearing journey by providing an action plan, encouragement, accountability and as much hand holding as needed.

Online Group Feng Shui Programs – If you're not ready for a private consultation but need more support and accountability, one of Kerri's online group programs might be right for you.

Speaking Engagements –Kerri is available to share her knowledge of feng shui and its benefits with your group.

Feng Shui Tips – Sign up for the Feng Shui Pathways newsletter to get regular Feng Shui tips and information on upcoming offerings delivered to your inbox. Subscribe to the Feng Shui Pathways YouTube channel for Feng Shui video tips.

Social Media – Follow Feng Shui Pathways on Facebook, Twitter, and YouTube

Join the "Feels Better. Flows Better. Living With Inspiration" Social Community!!

This Facebook community is a space to share inspirations for creating a home and family life that feels better and flows better. Feng shui is a big part of this as are other muses including aromatherapy, clutter clearing, organizing, living with what you love, minimalism, the law of attraction, and much, much more. It's a place for sharing and supporting anything that contributes to living an inspired and deliberate life. Search for the group on Facebook and request to join.

For specific inquiries, contact Kerri Miller directly

Email: Kerri@FengShuiPathways.com

Website: www.FengShuiPathways.com

ABOUT KERRI

Author photograph: © Sara Maida

Kerri Miller is the Founder of Feng Shui Path-ways. She's passionate about sharing the benefits of Feng Shui with others so they can be empowered to create spaces that feel better and flow better. Kerri believes that a space that feels good can ex-ponentially impact all areas of life in a positive way. This belief comes from her personal experiences in using Feng Shui, and watching many of her clients benefit from it too.

Kerri studied at the Western School of Feng Shui in 2004 and has been practicing as a consultant ever since. She lives in Massachusetts with her husband and two daughters. Kerri faithfully applies Feng Shui at home by blending many positive Chi items in with the abundance of stuffed animals and Barbie dolls ... And she's become adept at making sure everyone, and the chi, can move with ease and grace regardless of how big the laundry piles are!

Kerri brings the practicality of real, functional living into every area of her work. Using a com-bined knowledge of Feng Shui, aromatherapy, coaching, organizing, and space clearing, she em-powers clients to craft spaces that are comfortable, functional, supportive and inspiring. She of-fers private Feng Shui consultations on-site or by phone. She also facilitates several online group Feng Shui programs including "The Clutter Clearing Challenge" and "Applying Feng Shui Basics at Home".

To follow Kerri's blog, and for information about Feng Shui and Kerri's other offerings, visit www.FengShuiPathways.com.

Lightning Source UK Ltd.
Milton Keynes UK
UKHW050252140123
415281UK00005B/58